Mobile Research Methods

Opportunities and challenges of mobile research methodologies

Edited by
Daniele Toninelli, Robert Pinter and
Pablo de Pedraza

]u[

ubiquity press
London

Published by
Ubiquity Press Ltd.
6 Windmill Street
London W1T 2JB
www.ubiquitypress.com

First published 2015

Cover design by Amber MacKay
Images used in the cover design were sourced from
Pixabay and are licensed under CC0 Public Domain.
Main cover image: stokpic
Background cover image: Comfreak

Printed in the UK by Lightning Source Ltd.

ISBN (Paperback): 978-1-909188-53-2
ISBN (PDF): 978-1-909188-54-9
ISBN (EPUB): 978-1-909188-55-6
ISBN (Kindle): 978-1-909188-56-3

DOI: http://dx.doi.org/10.5334/bar

Suggested citation: Toninelli, D, Pinter, R and de Pedraza, P 2015 *Mobile
Research Methods: Opportunities and challenges of mobile research
methodologies*. London: Ubiquity Press. DOI: http://dx.doi.org/10.5334/bar.
License: CC-BY 4.0

To read the online open access version of this
book, either visit http://dx.doi.org/10.5334/bar
or scan this QR code with your mobile device:

Table of Contents

Supporting Institutions

COST (European Cooperation in Science and Technology, www.cost.eu) is a pan-European intergovernmental framework. Its mission is to enable break-through scientific and technological developments leading to new concepts and products and thereby contribute to strengthening Europe's research and innovation capacities.

This book is based upon work from COST Action, supported by COST (European Cooperation in Science and Technology).

COST is supported by the EU Framework Programme Horizon 2020

Contributing Institutions

UNIVERSITÀ DEGLI STUDI DI BERGAMO

Contributors

Ioannis Andreadis: Ioannis Andreadis is an assistant professor at the Aristotle University of Thessaloniki. In 2014 he was a Fulbright Visiting Scholar at the University of Michigan working on the establishment of the Hellenic National Election Studies. He is a member of the steering committees of the ECPR standing group on Public Opinion and Voting Behaviour in a Comparative Perspective and of the Comparative Candidates Survey and a collaborator of the Comparative Study of Electoral Systems. He is a specialist in political web surveys and the leader of the WebDataNet Task Force: Web Survey Paradata. He has published his findings in book chapters, academic journals and conference proceedings. For more details see: http://www.polres.gr/en/andreadis (john@auth.gr)

Christopher Antoun: Christopher Antoun is a PhD candidate in Survey Methodology at the Institute for Social Research at the University of Michigan. His research focuses on the application of mobile devices to the survey process. (antoun@umich.edu)

João Pedro Azevedo: João Pedro Azevedo is a Lead Economist at the World Bank in Washington. He currently works for the Poverty Global Practice in the European and Central Asia region, focusing on Central Asia and Turkey and leading the region's Statistics Team. João Pedro also leads the Global Solution Area on Poverty and Equity Measurement and Statistical Capacity from the Poverty Global Practice. João Pedro has focused much of his work on helping developing countries improve their systems for evidence-based decision making. He worked in Colombia, Brazil and the Dominican Republic for five years, and led important regional public efforts such as the Latin American & Caribbean Stats Team and the Latin American & Caribbean Monitoring and Evaluation Network. João Pedro brings solid and varied experience in applied econometrics to the fields of poverty and inequality issues. Before joining the World Bank, João Pedro served as the superintendent of monitoring and evaluation at the Secretary of Finance for the State of Rio de Janeiro and was a research fellow at the Brazilian Ministry of Planning's Institute of Applied Economic Research. He is a former chairman of the Latin American & Caribbean Network on Inequality and Poverty and holds a PhD in Economics. (jazevedo@worldbank.org)

Amparo Ballivián: Amparo Ballivián is a Lead Economist at the World Bank in Washington. She works in the World Bank's Data group and leads the Open Government Data working group at the World Bank and co-leads the World

Bank's Big Data working group. These are multidisciplinary groups that support developing and emerging countries' Open Data, Big Data and other data innovation initiatives. She also heads the Secretariat of the World Bank's Data Council. Amparo has had a rich experience in development operations since 1991, having managed several development projects in various economic areas in the Latin America, Caribbean and Africa regional groups of the World Bank. Between 2002 and 2006 she was the World Bank's Country Manager and Resident Representative in Nicaragua. Before joining the World Bank she worked in public service, academia, diplomatic posts and the private sector. She has held senior Government positions in Bolivia, including Minister of Housing and, subsequently, Chairman of the Board of National Customs of Bolivia. She obtained a PhD in econometrics and a Master's in Mathematical Economics from Rice University in Houston, Texas. (aballivian@worldbank.org)

Mick P. Couper: Mick P. Couper, PhD, is a Research Professor in the Survey Research Center at the University of Michigan's Institute for Social Research and in the Joint Program in Survey Methodology at the University of Maryland. He is the author of *Designing Effective Web Surveys* (Cambridge, 2008) and a co-author (with Roger Tourangeau and Frederick Conrad) of *The Science of Web Surveys* (Oxford, 2013), and he has co-authored a number of papers on various aspects of Web survey design, including mobile Web surveys (mcouper@umich.edu).

Will Durbin: Will Durbin has been at the World Bank since 2009, working on a variety of projects in the poverty and health sectors. His work has ranged from conducting poverty assessments, constructing human opportunity indexes and studying adolescent pregnancy in Latin America, to running capacity building sessions on the use of tablets in household surveys employing a new World Bank technique to measure household poverty with only a dozen questions. He studied Ethics, Politics and Economics at Yale University (2001) and holds a Master in Public Affairs from Princeton University (2009) with a focus on international development. He grew up in Needham, Massachusetts. (sdurbin@worldbank.org)

Germán Loewe: Germán Loewe holds a PhD in Mathematical Economics from the University of Barcelona. He founded Netquest in 2001 and is now its CEO. He also started collaborating with the Managerial Decision Sciences department at the IESE Business School, University of Navarra, in 2009, and is now Lecturer in Decision Analysis in its MBA program. His main research areas are intertemporal choice and web surveys.

Aigul Mavletova: Aigul Mavletova, PhD, is a senior lecturer at the National Research University Higher School of Economics, Russia. Her current research interests focus on data quality in web surveys and new technologies used in data collection processes. (amavletova@hse.ru)

Carlos Ochoa: Carlos Ochoa has an Engineering degree in Telecommunications (UPC, Barcelona) and has experience in consultancy, sales and product management. After having been Operations Director at Netquest, he is currently in charge of defining the marketing strategy of the company as its-Marketing and Innovation Director, as well as fostering innovation projects in the quality data collection area. He has been responsible for the design and operation of Netquest panels in 21 Latin American countries for the last eight years.

Pablo de Pedraza*: Pablo de Pedraza works at the Amsterdam Institute for Advanced labour Studies (AIAS, University of Amsterdam) and at the Applied Economics Department of the University of Salamanca. He conducts research in post-adjustment techniques in international labour-oriented web surveys, labour economics, job insecurity, life satisfaction and the use of web data in applied economics. He is the Chairman of WebDataNet (www.webdatanet. eu), an EU Cost Action network that brings together web data and mobile research experts from a variety of disciplines, aiming to address methodological issues of web-based data collection and foster its scientific usage by contributing to its theoretical and empirical foundations, stimulating its integration into the entire research process, and enhancing its integrity and legitimacy. Since 2005 he is a member of the WageIndicator Foundation: www.wageindicator.org. (p.dePedraza@uva.nl)

Robert Pinter*: Robert Pinter is an assistant professor at the Department of Information and Communication, Corvinus University of Budapest and is Head of Mobile Research at eNET Internet Research and Consulting Ltd., a Budapest-based research agency. He is an online research professional who has worked for Ipsos Interactive Services between 2008 and 2012 as online client service director in Hungary, then in the Czech Republic and Russia. Since 2013 he has been the leader of an online-mobile hybrid research system called 'VeVa' and has been responsible for the development of its smartphone research application. His teaching activities include online and mobile research methods and information society classes at Corvinus University, Hungary. He is the leader of the WebDataNet COST Action Task Force on Mobile Research. (robert. pinter@enet.hu)

Ray Poynter: Ray Poynter is the Managing Director of The Future Place, the founder of NewMR.org, and the author of *The Handbook of Online and Social Media Research* and *The Handbook of Mobile Market Research*. He has spent over 35 years in the market research industry and is a regular contributor to events and activities, including as the writer of a widely read blog. His professional activities include: editing ESOMAR's book *Answers to Contemporary Market Research Questions*, authoring content for the University of Georgia's MRII Principles of Marketing Research Course, and providing workshops for the UK's MRS and other bodies. ray.poynter@thefutureplace.com

Melanie Revilla: Melanie Revilla holds a PhD in Statistics and Survey Methodology from Pompeu Fabra University, Spain. She graduated from the Ecole nationale de la statistique et de l'administration économique (ENSAE-Paritech, France) and has a Master's in Economics from the Barcelona Graduate School of Economics (BGSE). She is currently a researcher at the Research and Expertise Centre for Survey Methodology (RECSM) and an adjunct professor at Pompeu Fabra University. Her main research interests are survey methodology, modes of data collection, web surveys, correction for measurement errors, and causal modeling. (melanie.revilla@upf.edu)

Ana Slavec: Ana Slavec is a PhD student at the University of Ljubljana and a research assistant at the Centre for Social Informatics at the Faculty of Social Sciences at the same university. She has worked as a survey methodologist on several national and international projects. Currently she is working on post-survey adjustments for the European Social Survey. She is also an active member of the WebDataNet COST network. Her main research interests are web surveys, dual-frame surveys, questionnaire development, data weighting, and social network analysis. In her dissertation she is researching the potential of language technologies to improve survey question wording. (ana.slavec@fdv. uni-lj.si)

Daniele Toninelli*: Daniele Toninelli is currently Assistant Professor of Statistics and Economics in the Department of Management, Economics and Quantitative Methods at the University of Bergamo (Italy). He graduated in Statistics (2003, University of Milan-Bicocca), and he has an MSc degree in Statistics for Marketing Research and Surveys (2004, University of Milan-Bicocca) and a PhD in Marketing for Enterprise Strategies (2009, University of Bergamo). His other work experience includes: working at PiTre S.r.l. (2000–2001), IBM Italia/ Celestica (1994–2001) and Multiplex Arcadia (2002–2003); and work as a PhD student / visiting researcher at Statistics Canada (2008, 2009, 2012–2013) and as a visiting researcher at the University of Ottawa (2012–2013). His teaching activities include teaching the following (main courses): Index Numbers Theory, Statistics for Financial Markets, Economics and Statistics for Marketing Research, Advanced Business Statistics, and Advanced Probability and Statistics for Finance. His main research interests and publication areas are: survey & web survey methodology, price indexes, and statistics for finance. (daniele.toninelli@ unibg.it)

*indicates the co-editors of this volume

Competing interests

CO is the R&D director of Netquest. GL is the CEO of Netquest. All other authors declare that they have no competing interests

Mobile Research Methods: Possibilities and Issues of a New Promising Way of Conducting Research

Robert Pinter*, Daniele Toninelli[†] and
Pablo de Pedraza[‡]

*eNet, Hungary, robert.pinter@enet.hu,
†University of Bergamo, Italy, daniele.toninelli@unibg.it,
‡University of Amsterdam, Netherlands, P.dePedraza@uva.nl

Abstract

This chapter introduces the WebDataNet group as the development framework of this book. It also presents the most relevant themes regarding the Mobile Research Methods in different research areas and the opportunities, issues and state of the art of mobile research. Finally, it summarizes the book structure and content.

Keywords

WebDataNet, mobile research, research methods, book introduction

Background of the book: the scientific framework of WebDataNet & the Task Force on Mobile Research

Nowadays, in human daily activity, data are constantly flowing through cameras, via internet, satellites, radio frequencies, sensors, private appliances, cars, mobile phones, tablets and the like. Among all the tools currently used, mobile

---

How to cite this book chapter:
Pinter, R, Toninelli, D and de Pedraza, P. 2015. Mobile Research Methods: Possibilities and Issues of a New Promising Way of Conducting Research. In: Toninelli, D, Pinter, R & de Pedraza, P (eds.) *Mobile Research Methods: Opportunities and Challenges of Mobile Research Methodologies*, Pp. 1–10. London: Ubiquity Press. DOI: http://dx.doi.org/10.5334/bar.a. License: CC-BY 4.0.

devices (especially mobile phones, smartphones and tablets) are the most wide-spread, thanks also to their easier portability. People use them more and more often in all kind of areas of everyday life. Even in the developing world, more and more people conduct activities via the Internet. For instance, people use the Internet for shopping, reading newspapers, participating in forums, completing and making surveys, communicating with friends and making new ones, filing their tax returns, getting involved in politics, purchasing things or looking for information before purchasing offline. Mobile devices allow a wide range of heterogeneous activities and, as a result, they have great potential in terms of the different types of data that can be collected using them. In fact, the use of these devices as tools for data collection is gaining popularity. Mobile devices affect research as well, and the new situation provides, above all, an opportunity that applied research is only starting to explore. First, mobile usage already influences the applicability of traditional research methods. The representativeness of traditional landline samples is challenged by mobile-only respondents. Mobiles or tablets may be used in Computer-Assisted Personal Interviews (CAPI) instead of laptops. Respondents in online surveys planned for a PC environment may rather use mobile devices. Secondly, mobile devices can be used independently in mobile internet-based surveys, in mobile ethnography, in mobile diary, in location-based research or in passive measurement.

Aiming at exploring the many ways in which the Data Revolution[1] could benefit social sciences methods, WebDataNet[2] was created in 2009 by a small group of researchers willing to focus the discussion on web-based data collection methods. Thanks to the support of the European Union programme for the Coordination of Science and Technology (COST),[3] WebDataNet has become an ever-growing, unique, multidisciplinary network that has brought together leading web-based data collection experts from several institutions, disciplines, and relevant backgrounds from more than 35 different countries (Steinmetz et al. 2012; Steinmetz et al. 2014; WebDataNet 2010).

The fundamental goal of WebDataNet is to address the methodological issues of web-based data collection and to foster its scientific usage. In order to fulfil this goal WebDatNet´s scientific structure is designed to follow a bottom-up approach. The framework consists of three general Working Groups (WGs): WG1 - Quality issues, WG2 - Innovation and WG3 - Implementation. Researchers can organize their Task Forces (TFs) within these WGs to foster their research interest by building collaborations and synergies with other

---

[1] Data emerging from all activities developed by means of mobile devices, together with an increase and proliferation of digital storage capacity, have activated discussion about concepts such as Big Data (Couper 2013; Mayer-Schonberger & Cukier 2013; Snijders, Matzat & Reips 2012), Organic Data (Groves 2011), the Data Revolution (United Nations 2013) or the Digital data tsunami (Prewitt 2013).

[2] For more information on WebDataNet, see www.webdatanet.eu.

[3] For more information on COST, see www.cost.eu.

researchers.[4] WebDataNet has supported more than 30 TFs within the topic of web-based data collection methods and implementations by organizing meetings, workshops, training schools and supporting short-term scientific research visits. This book was written mainly thanks to the collaborations activated in the framework of the WebDataNet´s Task Force # 19 (TF19). This Task Force focuses on mobile research and is coordinated by Robert Pinter. It was founded in Mannheim, in March 2013, by a group of researchers interested in the topic. TF19's fundamental goal has been to systematically compare mobile research to traditional methods and to investigate it as an independent research method.

The task force on mobile research was also the main actor in one of the Web-DataNet meetings, organized in Larnaca (Cyprus) in April 2014.[5] A conference on Mobile Research took place in Larnaca, involving many members of the TF19. The potential of a clearly crucial topic, the major role that mobile devices could play in the future of research and the determination of TF19 members gave rise to the idea of developing a book on mobile research. This book includes works that are a further development of preliminary presentations made in the Larnaca Conference, but it also collects works that discuss results of new research activities.

Book target and contribution to the field: the importance of mobile research

This book, *Mobile Research Methods*, is focusing on the study of the use of mobile devices in various research contexts. The impact of mobile devices in research is a relatively recent and still partly unexplored topic. This book mainly aims at deeply studying this topic and at providing readers with a more detailed and updated knowledge, compared to what is currently available in the literature. This is done considering different aspects: main methodological possibilities and issues, comparison and integration with more traditional survey modes or ways of participating in research, quality of collected data, main characteristics of the new kind of respondents (unintended mobile respondents), use of mobile in commercial market research, study of the representativeness of studies based only on the mobile-population, analysis of the current spread of mobile devices in several countries, and so on. Thus, the book also provides the readers with interesting research findings that include a wide range of countries and contexts.

Many books have already been published about mobile research in the last few years, for example: Maxl, Döring & Wallisch 2009; Häder, Häder & Kühne 2012; Poynter, Williams & York 2014; Appleton 2014. However, our book,

---

[4] For more information on the scientific framework of WebDataNet, see: http://webdatanet.cbs. dk/index.php/test/scientific-coordination.

[5] http://webdatanet.cbs.dk/index.php/data/117-next-mc-meeting-cyprus-2014.

Mobile Research Methods, is more general than Appleton's one, more up to date than Maxl, Döring and Wallisch's book, oriented to a wider audience than Poynter, Williams and York's book and broader than Häder, Häder and Kühne's book, which focuses more on traditional landline phone surveys. This book is different thanks to the fact that its development involved the multinational and inter-disciplinary team of WebDataNet, with team members from different research fields, such as social sciences, survey methodology, applied statistics, and marketing and behavioral sciences (Steinmetz et al. 2014).

The mobile research phenomenon is still mostly unexplored, considering its recent worldwide spreading, and it involves several research disciplines: thus, a more complete, more in-depth and more updated study of the phenomenon is needed that considers a variety of points of view and approaches. New methodological questions arise with mobile phone research, and we need to explore these main research questions. For example, what is the relation between mobile mode and other, more traditional methods? What are the advantages and disadvantages of mobile data collection? What is the reliability and validity of research data collected by means of mobile phones? What is the quality of mobile-gathered data? How does mobile research affect coverage issues and nonresponse bias and what is the difference between mobile and non-mobile respondents? This book is most useful for those readers who are interested in online research methods, especially in online panel research. It can be also interesting for readers who plan to use mobile device applications for research purposes.

The potential readership of *Mobile Research Methods* includes: researchers and practitioners; users of web panel data and of telephone surveys data; survey methodologists and web and mobile survey designers; market research professionals; policy-makers, researchers and practitioners working on poverty measurement and survey data innovations; and survey methodology students and advanced research courses' students (e.g. advanced university courses, PhD, master or specialized courses). This book can also be helpful to research and data collection companies, online panel providers and other research institutions (in private or public sector). Hence this book is not only a teaching material, it can also be valuable for public or private research institutions that are involved in the development of any kind of research.

Structure of the book

This book has three sections. The first part includes an introduction to the use of mobile devices in research and to its main potentialities (e.g. the integration with more traditional survey modes) and issues. The second part mainly focuses on the quality of data collected by means of mobile devices, also making a comparison with other survey modes. The third part studies mobile web survey participation, analyzing the spread of mobile devices in different countries and the willingness of participating in surveys by means of these devices; it also proposes new methods of data collection based on smartphone applications.

The **first part** of the book starts with the chapter entitled '*The Utilization of Mobile Technology and Approaches in Commercial Market Research*'. In this chapter, **Ray Poynter** underlines the importance of mobile technology, introducing its main uses in various research contexts, together with the current most common approaches. For example, **Poynter** classifies research projects according to the use of mobile devices. Introducing mobile technology, the author makes a comparison with an iceberg ('the less visible is much larger than the visible'). By means of this comparison, he explains how the projects in which mobile devices are used represent only a small fraction of the role that mobile research has been playing in the last few years. The author's approach focuses, in particular, on commercial research, also digging out the main issues involved in the use of mobile technology.

Even if the mobile technologies are more and more frequently used in research, the mobile research methods still have to be fully explored and studied. Several new emerging quality issues are causing concerns, and a lot of research projects have started to study the quality of data collected using mobile devices. One of these projects, aimed at dealing with some of these challenges, is the LAC (Listening to Latin America and the Caribbean) project. The project is described in the chapter written by **Amparo Ballivian, João Pedro Azevedo and Will Durbin** ('*Using Mobile Phones for High-Frequency Data Collection*'). The main objective of the study is to test the reliability and validity of survey data collected by means of mobile phones, focusing on CATI surveys. In this framework, the research team reached important empirical results. The authors are now able to provide readers with open-source materials ('data, reports, guidelines, software, user manuals, video and other materials') that can be extremely useful to both plan and manage mobile surveys (and, in particular, mobile phone surveys). In this chapter, the authors also underline the main advantages of mobile technology together with its main issues.

It is clear that when a new research methodology arises, new issues emerge at the same time. First of all it is necessary to understand if and how the new methodology can be successfully integrated with other more traditional data collection methods. From this perspective, the spread of mobile devices can be seen, for example, as an effective help in compensating for the drop of coverage rates in landline telephone surveys. Nevertheless, the inclusion of mobile phone participation causes new arising issues, or confirms issues commonly found with other more traditional data collection methods. In the chapter entitled ' *An Overview of Mobile CATI Issues in Europe*', **Ana Slavec and Daniele Toninelli** study the mobile-CATI fieldwork, summarizing and reviewing some of the main challenges that mobile phone usage causes to survey participation. The authors mainly focus on issues linked to legal and ethical rules, to the coverage of the target population, to the sample selection or to the main sources of error (nonresponse, measurement) and introduce the readers to some adjustment procedures. The depicted situation is strongly varying according to the national/regional contexts and legislations. Nevertheless, some general rules and recommendations can be identified and can be followed in planning and conducting research, in order to at least reduce the impact of the different issues on the quality of collected data.

On the one hand, the integration of mobile participation in other more traditional survey modes can help reduce or compensate for arising issues. On the other hand it also becomes necessary to make a comparison between data collected by means of the new technologies and data collected using more traditional research methods. Within this perspective, the **second part** of the book is mainly focused on the study of the quality of collected data. Are the new methods more effective, fast, precise, etc.? How much can be gained from using mobile methods in research? Is mobile data collection more competitive? Can it help in obtaining data of higher quality? **Ioannis Andreadis**, in the chapter entitled '*Comparison of Response Times between Desktop and Smartphone Users*', focuses on the completion time in the framework of web surveys. The main objective, considering both the item response times and the total response times, is to test if both types of response times can be substantially reduced using mobile methods of data collection (smartphones, in this case), in comparison to a more traditional fixed-PC survey participation.

The quality of data collected using mobile devices in the context of web surveys is also the central topic of the chapter written by **Aigul Mavletova and Mick Couper**, '*A Meta-Analysis of Breakoff Rates in Mobile Web Surveys*'. The starting point is a meta-analysis based on several studies done on both probability-based and non-probability-based panels. In particular, the authors study the breakoff rates obtained in mobile web surveys subject to various experimental settings. Among other factors, they also take into account the optimization of the survey for mobile participation. The authors' findings also provide readers with some suggestions about the setting of web surveys that can help in reducing the breakoff rates.

The quality of data collected using mobile devices is also strictly linked to the characteristics of the population that can be potentially involved in a research/ survey project. This is the focus point of the **third part** of the book. According to some preliminary studies (e.g. Fuchs & Busse 2009), there are characteristics differentiating the population owning a mobile device (the so-called 'mobile early adopters'). But these differences, despite being confirmed by more recent studies (e.g. de Bruijne & Wijnant 2014), are becoming more and more narrow, thanks to the quick spread of mobile devices among the general population. Nevertheless, at this point, it is not clear whether there are big differences between people that have access to mobile web and people that are mostly fixed-PC or laptop web users. Moreover, the situation is evolving very quickly. Thus, further updated studies are needed. In these circumstances, the following three chapters focus on the study of the population involved in using mobile devices in research or survey projects.

The first of the three chapters ('*Who Are the Internet Users, Mobile Internet Users, and Mobile-mostly Internet Users?: Demographic Differences across Internet-use Subgroups in the U.S.*', by **Christopher Antoun**) analyzes the characteristics of some specific groups of respondents by means of data coming from a Pew telephone survey. The study starts from the premise that the quality of collected data can be affected by allowing or not allowing a potential respondent to participate to a survey using a mobile device, on one hand, and by the potential respondent's decision to participate or not by means of a specific device, on the other hand. In **Antoun**'s chapter some of the main characteristics (both demographic and non-demographic) of different subgroups of respondents are studied. These groups are defined considering: the use of Internet, the mobile web use (conditional on the Internet use) and the prevailing mobile vs fixed-PC usage (conditional to the mobile web use). The author's approach is helpful in defining possible coverage issues and in detecting if and how the mobile respondents can differ from non-mobile respondents.

Furthermore, as also underlined in the previous chapters, when a mobile survey is planned there are two relevant points that have to be taken into consideration: the availability of mobile devices among the units of the target population and the willingness of respondents to participate by means of these devices.

The chapter written by **Melanie Revilla, Daniele Toninelli, Carlos Ochoa and Germán Loewe**, entitled '*Who Has Access to Mobile Devices in an Online Opt-in Panel? An Analysis of Potential Respondents for Mobile Surveys*', mainly deals with the first of these two points. This study is based on data collected by a non-probability-based panel. The coverage level of mobile devices (mainly smartphones and tablets) considering both the devices owned by potential respondents and the devices that they have at their disposal (even if not-owned) is explored in several countries. It is clear that the increasing spread of the mobile devices availability directly affects the quality of collected data and the representativeness of the surveyed population. This chapter highlights that there is often more than one device at the respondents' disposal. Thus, the necessity to study a) what pushes respondents to choose a certain device for the survey participation (their preferences) and b) the characteristics of the respondents that own a certain kind of device (or a combination of them) clearly emerges.

Regarding the preferences of respondents, an interesting analysis is presented by **Robert Pinter** in his chapter: '*Willingness of Online Access Panel Members to Participate in Smartphone Application-Based Research*'. Given the quickly spreading penetration of mobile devices, the author studies the use of smartphone applications in research. The use of downloaded or pre-installed smartphone applications is an additional and new emerging way of conducting online research. It represents our 'look to the future', considering that it is not currently as well developed and well spread as the more traditional mobile web survey participation. Moreover, this new methodology includes an offline participation option (responses are only synchronized if internet access is available). Thus, it requires a further and more specifically developed study of the population that can be potentially involved in terms of both its characteristics and its members' willingness to participate in application-based research of different kinds. This last chapter and its findings provides further details about one of the potentially most interesting evolutions of research conducted by means of mobile devices in the future.

Acknowledgements

Editors and authors would like to acknowledge the contribution of the COST Action IS1004: the networking activities that the project were able to start and stimulate made possible the realization of this book. The author would also like to acknowledge WebDataNet, the European network for web-based data collection (COST Action IS1004, http://webdatanet.cbs.dk/), for giving birth to our collaboration and for funding the publication of this book. Moreover, we would like to thank Christopher Antoun, Aigul Mavletova, Melanie Revilla and Ana Slavec for contributing to the development of this chapter.

References

Appleton, E. (2014). In the Moment. Perspectives on Mobile Market Research. Edward Appleton.

Couper, M. P. (2013). Is the sky falling? New technology, changing media, and the future of surveys. *Survey Research Methods, 7*(3), 145–156.

de Bruijne, M., & Wijnant, A. (2014). Mobile Response in Web Panels, *Social Science Computer Review, 32*(6), 728–742. DOI: http://dx.doi.org/10.1177/0894439314525918

Fuchs, M., & Busse, B. (2009). The coverage bias of mobile web surveys across European countries. *International Journal of Internet Science, 4*, 21–33.

Groves, R. (2011). Three eras of survey research. *Public Opinion Quarterly, 75*(5), 861–871. DOI: http://dx.doi.org/10.1093/poq/nfr057

Häder, S., Häder, M., & Kühne, M. (2012). Telephone Surveys in Europe. Springer. DOI: http://dx.doi.org/10.1007/978-3-642-25411-6

Maxl, E., Döring, N., & Wallisch, A. (2009). Mobile Market Research. Herbert Von Halem Verlag.

Mayer-Schonberger, V., & Cukier, K. (2013). Big data A Revolution That Will Transform How we Live, Work and Think. Boston, New York: An Eamon Dolan Book, Houghton Mifflin Harcourt.

Poynter, R., Williams, N., & York, S. (2014). The Handbook of Mobile Market Research: Tools and Techniques for Market Researchers. John Wiley & Sons Ltd.

Prewitt, K. (2013). The 2012 Morris Hansen lecture: Thank you Morris, et al., for Westat, et al. *Journal of Official Statistics, 29*(2), 223–231. DOI: http://dx.doi.org/10.2478/jos-2013-0018

Snijders, C., Matzat, U., & Reips, U.-D. (2012). 'Big Data': Big gaps of knowledge in the field of Internet science. *International Journal of Internet Science, 7*, 1–5.

Steinmetz, S., Kaczmirek, L., De Pedraza, P., Reips, U.-D., Tijdens, K., Lozar Manfreda, K., Rowland, L., Serrano, F., Vidakovic, M., Vogel, C., Belchior, A., Berzelak, J., Biffignandi, S., Birgegard, A., Cachia, E., Callegaro, M., Camilleri, P. J., Campagnolo, G. M., Cantijoch, M., Cheikhrouhou, N., Constantin, D., Dar, R., David, S., De Leeuw, E., Doron, G., Fernandez-Macias, E., Finnemann, N. O., Foulonneau, M., Fornara, N., Fuchs, M., Funke, F., Gibson, R., Grceva, S., Haraldsen, G., Jonsdottir, G., Kahanec, M., Kissau, K., Kolsrud, K., Lenzner, T., Lesnard, L., Margetts, H., Markov, Y., Milas, G., Mlacic, B., Moga, L. M., Neculita, M., Popescu, A. I., Ronkainen, S., Scherpenzeel, A., Selkala, A., Kalgraff Skjak, K., Slavec, A., Staehli, M. E., Thorsdottir, F., Toninelli, D., Vatrapu, R., Vehovar, V., Villacampa Gonzalez, A., Winer, B. (2012). WEBDATANET. A web-based data collection, methodological challenges, solutions and implementations. *International Journal of Internet Science, 7*(1), 78–89. Retrieved from http://www.ijis.net/ijis7_1/ijis7_1_supplement_pre.html.

Steinmetz, S., Slavec, A., Tijdens, K., Reips, U.-D., de Pedraza, P., Popescu, A., Belchior, A., Birgegard, A., Bianchi, A., Ayalon, A., Selkala, A., Villacampa, A., Winer B. (D.), Mlacic, B., Vogel, C., Gravem, D., Avello, D.G., Constantin, D., Toninelli, D., Troitino, D., Horvath, D., De Leeuw, E., Oren, E., Fernandez-Macias, E., Thorsdottir, F., Ortega, F., Funke, F., Campagnolo, G. M., Milas, G., Grünwald, C., Jonsdottir, G., Haraldsen, G., Doron, G., Margetts, H., Miklousic, I., Andreadis, I., Berzelak, J., Angelovska, J., Schrittwieser, K., Kissau, K., Manfreda, K. L., Kolsrud, K., Skjak, K. K., Tsagarakis, K., Kaczmirek, L., Lesnard, L., Moga, L. M., Teixeira, L. L., Plate, M., Kozak, M., Fuchs, M., Callegaro, M., Cantijoch. M., Kahanec, M., Stopa, M., Staehli, E. M., Neculita, M., Ivanovic, M., Foulonneau, M., Cheikhrouhou, N., Fornara, N., Finnemann, N. O., Zajc, N., Nyirő, N., Louca, P., Osse, P., Mavrikiou, P., Gibson, R., Vatrapu, R., Dar, R., Pinter, R., Torres, R. M., Douhou, S., Biffignandi, S., Grceva, S., David S., Ronkainen, S., Csordas, T., Lenzner, T., Vesteinsdottir, V., Vehovar, V., & Markov, Y. (2014). WEBDATANET: Innovation and Quality in Web-Based Data Collection. *International Journal of Internet Science, 9*(1). Retrieved from http://www.ijis.net/ijis9_1/ijis9_1_supplement_pre.html.

United Nations. (2013). *A New Global Partnership: Eradicate poverty and transform economies through sustainable development.* The Report of the

High-Level Panel of Eminent Persons on the Post-2015 Development Agenda. Retrieved from http://www.un.org/sg/management/pdf/HLP_ P2015_Report.pdf

WebDataNet. (2010). *Memorandum of Understanding for the implementation of a European Concerted Research Action designated as COST Action IS1004: WEBDATANET: web based data-collection – methodological challenges, solutions and implementations.* Retrieved from http://webdatanet.cbs.dk/ images/presentations/mou%20is1004-webdatanet.pdf

The Utilization of Mobile Technology and Approaches in Commercial Market Research

Ray Poynter

The Future Place, UK,
ray.poynter@thefutureplace.com

Abstract

This chapter provides an overview of how mobile devices, technology, and approaches are currently being utilized by commercial market research. The chapter defines what it means by 'mobile' and highlights the difference between the 'visible' (projects where the use of mobile is seen as a core part of the project) and the 'less visible' (for example mobile devices being used to take part in online surveys designed for PCs). In commercial research the visible mobile projects get most of the attention in the media and at conferences, but the less visible is much larger in terms of the amount of data collected and the money spent.

The chapter then goes on to review the key uses of mobile, for example: web surveys, CATI, CAPI, mobile apps, passive data collection, in-the-moment research, and location-based research. The chapter next looks at the issues facing the use of mobile market research, such as the impact on the results, ethical issues, and the balance between the use of web-based and app-based approaches. The chapter concludes by looking at the near future.

Keywords

Commercial market research, market adoption, CATI, mCAPI, location-based research, in-the-moment

---

How to cite this book chapter:
Poynter, R. 2015. The Utilization of Mobile Technology and Approaches in Commercial Market Research. In: Toninelli, D, Pinter, R & de Pedraza, P (eds.) *Mobile Research Methods: Opportunities and Challenges of Mobile Research Methodologies*, Pp. 11–20. London: Ubiquity Press. DOI: http://dx.doi.org/10.5334/bar.b. License: CC-BY 4.0.

Mobile, finally the 'next big thing'

Market researchers have been talking about 'mobile' as the next big thing for over a decade, but following several false dawns the delay in it arriving was beginning to seem endless (Baker 2011). However, by 2014 it was widely agreed that in the world of commercial market research mobile approaches had arrived in widespread and important ways (Poynter 2014).

In reviewing the role of mobile approaches in the domain of commercial research the analogy of an iceberg is useful. The visible part is interesting, but the substantial part is below the surface, and both parts are addressed in this review. This review outlines the current utilization of mobile approaches in commercial market research, highlights the key issues, and sets out some of the likely developments in the near future.

Defining 'mobile'

In the context of commercial market research the term 'mobile' encompasses the following types of devices:

- Mobile phones, which are often subdivided into smartphones and feature phones. Feature phones are sometimes further subdivided into those which have some form of internet capability (e.g. a browser and a mobile connection) and those that can only utilize voice and/or text based systems such as SMS.
- Tablets, for example iPads, which are in turn subdivided by size and whether they are connected to the mobile phone network or whether they rely solely on Wi-Fi.
- Wearable devices such as smart watches and Google Glass.

The demarcation between these devices is not always clear. The so-called 'phablet' is a smartphone that is larger than a typical mobile phone, but smaller than most tablets, combining the benefits of both. The term 'phablet' is a combination of the words 'PHone' and 'tABLET'. At the other end of the scale many of the wearables, such as Google Glass, require a mobile phone in order to be useful; in essence the wearable is a peripheral device to the smartphone.

The technology of mobile tends to be utilized by researchers in two ways: active and passive. Active use is when the user, the research participant, uses their phone to take part in the research; for example, they complete a survey on their tablet or use their mobile phone to take pictures or capture videos. Passive use is where researchers gather information about research participants automatically, using data collected from the mobile device, for example using GPS to track the movement of the phone or apps to monitor media consumption.

The visible and the less visible

The visible profile of mobile approaches in commercial market research includes: conferences devoted to mobile market research (for example Merlien's MRMW series of conferences and ESOMAR's Digital Dimensions conferences), courses in mobile market research (for example the University of Georgia's Principles of Mobile Market Research course , and the workshops held by a variety of organizations, such as ESOMAR and the UK's MRS), the growth in products facilitating mobile market research (for example mobile optimized surveys from companies like Confirmit and Decipher), and the growth in dedicated services (such as the global mobile solutions provided by Jana.com and OnDevice).

In August 2014, the visible aspect of the mobile revolution was brought into sharp definition by the publication by Wiley of *The Handbook of Mobile Market Research*, written by Poynter, Williams and York and supported by ESOMAR, creating the standard reference for the market research industry.

The less visible aspect of mobile market research relates to the large amount of commercial work that is already being conducted via mobile devices. For example, something like 25–30% of online surveys in 2014 are being attempted by people using mobile devices; a large proportion of CATI interviews are being completed via mobile phones; there has been substantial growth in the use of mobiles with CAPI ('mCAPI'); and new versions of traditional research are being invented, for example mobile auto-ethnography (Poynter, Williams & York 2014). The figure of 25–30% is in accord with figures reporting on overall mobile internet usage in the general worldwide population, which is also about 25% (Revilla et al. 2014).

This dichotomy of visible and less visible approaches has led to the slightly surreal paradox of some people talking about mobile as a purely theoretical phenomenon, whilst others are engaged in large-scale mobile projects. This contrast highlights potential problems for legislators and regulators in terms of updating laws, rules, and guidelines in a world where practice is moving ahead of considered theory.

The potential problems created by the dichotomy of visible and invisible approaches are well illustrated by the use of mobiles by respondents taking part in online surveys. The term 'unintentional mobile' has been coined to describe the situation where surveys that were not designed or intended for mobile are being taken by people using tablets or mobile phones (Peterson 2012). Whilst it appears that 25% to 30% of survey attempts are from people using mobiles, it would appear only about 2% of surveys have been optimized for mobile (Chadwick 2014). The topic of optimizing for mobile highlights the dilemma that failing to optimize for mobile could result in unwanted impacts on the data and on the relationship with respondents, but optimizing for mobile could also have an impact on the results. For example, failing to optimize for mobile could lead to more respondents finding the survey burdensome, and therefore more of them may break off from the survey. Other respondents might persevere with the survey but not be able to see the items in the way intended, leading to changes in the data and data quality issues. However, optimizing for mobile (for example shortening questions or changing the question types) might result in mode effects.

Current utilization of mobile technologies in market research

Mobile technologies are being used in commercial market research in the following ways:

- Taking part in online surveys via web browsers on mobile devices. In developed economies this category is largely restricted to smartphones; in the developing economies the use of feature phones with web access is often an important element.
- Taking part in telephone surveys (CATI) from mobile phones. In the developed markets this has been a gradual trend; in the developing markets mobile phones have outnumbered landlines for many years.
- Mobile devices being used by interviewers, moving from CAPI to mCAPI.
- Taking part in surveys via apps on mobile devices.
- Taking part in the collection of diary and ethnographic data using mobile devices.
- The collection of passive data, such as device usage and location.

Web surveys

According to ESOMAR (2014), online surveys is the most widely used data collection mode in terms of spend. Online research is typically conducted on people who are using the internet via a browser. Originally this tended to mean that online surveys were associated with PCs. However, recent reports suggest that about 25–30% of online surveys are being attempted by people using mobile devices. This means that it is important that researchers tackle the issue of device heterogeneity, dealing with PCs, tablets, and mobile phones.

The hot topic in commercial market research is around the need to be device agnostic, the aim being to allow the research participants to be free to use whatever device suits them, to increase response rates, broaden the pool of who is surveyed, and increase engagement. Note, there is a widespread belief in commercial market research circles that increasing engagement is a good thing. However, there are those who consider the benefits of engagement to be overstated and the problems (for example mode effects) to be understated (Downes-Le Guin et al. 2012).

CATI and mobiles

In the developed markets, CATI, and in particular RDD, was developed in the context of landlines. This assumption of landline use had several advantages, including cost (ringing landlines tends to be cheaper than ringing mobile phones) and the ability to target calls by geographic region. However, there has been a major growth in the number of people who do not have a landline. For example, the US CDC estimated that in 2013 over 40% of US homes were wireless only (Blumberg & Luke 2014). This growth in wireless-only homes has resulted in CATI having to deal with mobile phones, which has raised several issues, including:

- The extra costs of calling mobiles.
- The difficulties in targeting mobiles by geographic regions.
- The problems in combining a sample frame of landlines with a sample frame of mobile devices.
- Legal restrictions in how mobiles can be contacted (for example, many countries ban the use of auto-dialers and predictive dialers for mobiles).
- Potential mode effects; for example, will people be less likely to respond on mobile, will surveys need to be shorter, will the context within which people are answering the mobile phone impact the data (e.g. will a survey at home elicit a different response from a survey on a bus), and will the quality of the connection impact the experience and/or the results?

In the developing markets mobile devices have been key to telephone interviewing for longer than in the developed markets. This has been due to the relative scarcity of landlines in the least developed markets, and the relative abundance of mobile phones.

mCAPI

Computer-assisted personal interviewing (CAPI) has been in decline for many years, largely because of the growth in online surveys. However, mobile devices (both mobile phones and tablets) are giving it new life. In the developed markets tablets are being used to conduct location-based satisfaction surveys, utilizing the device as a multi-faceted aid to the interviewer, as well as a data collection device.

In the less developed markets mobiles (both phones and tablets) are facilitating a move away from paper questionnaires, a change that online surveys had not yet been able to achieve, because of issues around access to the internet, internet reliability, and in some cases literacy.

Mobile apps

The term 'mobile apps' refers to software that resides on a mobile device, occasionally pre-loaded, sometimes downloaded from a website, but typically downloaded from an app store, such as Apple's App Store or Android's Google Play.

Apps can be used in the context of online surveys, but they open up several other possibilities too, such as:

- Surveys when the internet is not available.
- Surveys which can access the features of the device, such as location or usage.
- Passive data collection.
- Push activities, where the activity (e.g. a survey) is initiated by the phone rather than relying on a message (e.g. an email or SMS) from the researcher.

It is likely to be some time before researchers come to a settled view on the merits of apps versus online solutions, with changes in technology and changes in utilization both impacting the final outcome.

Passive data collection

Passive data collection is where the device, for example a smartphone, is collecting information about the user without the user having to specifically enter information. In general, passive data can measure where the phone has been, what environmental factors (e.g. sound, other devices, or light) were detected, and what the phone has been used for. Combinations of these three elements can then be used to make inferences about the owner of the device.

In the world of commercial market research this process is predicated on informed consent from the research participant – this is less true of some other commercial uses of passive data collection, as was highlighted by some of the problems faced by Apple and Google about their tracking and collection of passive data.

Passive data collection is usually based on the use of apps. The research opportunities range from ad hoc qualitative projects through to large-scale projects, for example the steps being taken by Nielsen to measure media consumption.

'In-the-moment' research

Whilst the largest uses of mobile at the moment are online surveys, telephone surveys, and mCAPI, the biggest field of interest appears to be in the area of 'in-the-moment' research.

In-the-moment research relates to collecting research participants' views and reactions at the time they experience something, for example capturing responses during a shopping trip, whilst on a journey, or when entering a specific location.

The key driver for in-the-moment research relates to the growing awareness and acceptance that people's memories are unreliable. Surveys that ask people to remember which brands of soft drink they have consumed over the last 30 days, or why they chose that specific toothpaste, or how they felt when the train was late are collecting post-rationalized reasons about badly remembered events that the respondents were barely aware of at the time they happened.

It is widely felt that in-the-moment research can collect more accurate information by collecting it at the time when the event happens. It can be more accurate because it is contemporaneous and it can be more accurate because it can collect some of the information automatically (such as date, time, location etc.)

However, most in-the-moment research also represents a major change in the research paradigm. A traditional survey is a relatively controlled research experiment; the researcher creates the instrument, and the respondent completes it. However, in most forms of in-the-moment research the respondent is, to a greater or lesser extent, a collaborator in the research. The respondent carries the research medium with them, often in the form of an app downloaded onto their phone. The respondent is responsible for entering the responses. If photos or videos are included, the respondent is responsible for choosing the subject, the angle, the lighting, and numerous other factors that will impact the interpretation of the data.

Location-based research

Location-based research uses the location of the respondent as part of the data and as a method of triggering research exercises, such as surveys. The two key elements of location-based research are:

- Geo-tracking, i.e. identifying the routes taken by research respondents.
- Geofencing, or creating a boundary around a location (such as a specific retailer), recording when a respondent crosses the boundary (either entering or leaving the specified location), and triggering a research activity (such as a survey).

Most of the early interest in location-based research centered on GPS. GPS uses satellites to locate the mobile phone. However, GPS has several disadvantages, including the need for GPS to be enabled on the phone, the need to locate satellites (which tends to mean it does not work indoors), and the limited accuracy of phone-based GPS systems (which typically means that location systems cannot tell which specific store somebody entered).

Most of the current interest in location-based techniques is focused on beacons, and in particularly the Apple iBeacon. A beacon is placed in a specific location, such as a store or even a specific location within a store, and emits a signal (for example using Bluetooth LE). Beacons work by linking a smartphone to a location, recording when the phone arrives near the beacon and when the phone moves away from the beacon.

Another location-based approach is to identify where people are from the cell towers used to connect mobile phones to the phone network. This system is only available via the phone operators and is the source of several privacy concerns, but companies such as WEVE in the UK (a joint venture of three major mobile phone operators: EE, O2, and Vodafone) are making this route commercially available.

Key issues around mobile market research

Mobile market research is growing rapidly (GRIT 2014), taking a growing share of current approaches, and creating new opportunities. However, the changes are creating and highlighting a number of issues that need to be resolved, some by research-on-research and some by philosophical review and discussion.

Key issues include:

- Do the new approaches impact the results? And, if a new method changes the results, are they better, worse, or just different (and if different, what are the differences)?
- The drift in the use of mobile research is towards devices running Android and Apple iOS (i.e. towards smartphones and tablets) – this raises concerns that owners of older phones will be disregarded and discounted, in turn raising concerns about how to ensure that research is inclusive.
- Informed consent, which divides into two key questions: 1) How do we ensure that people are genuinely aware of what they are consenting to, especially in the area of passive data collection and where data is linked across multiple sources? 2) What about the rights of third-parties, for example people captured in photos and videos?
- What should the balance be between web surveys, app-based surveys, qualitative approaches, and passive data collection?
- How should methods be adapted to make best use of mobile technologies? For example, do surveys need to be shorter, do questions need to be simpler, and how best to use a smaller screen?
- How do the choices made impact the comparability of the results compared with research via more traditional devices?

Researchers should be aware that the field of mobile market research is highly dynamic, which means that the picture is continually evolving. Opportunities and challenges arise from changes in technology, legislation, commerce, and society. Researchers working with mobile research need to keep themselves up to date.

The near future

The rate of change in the utilization of mobile devices in market research shows no sign of diminishing. Key developments over the next few years are likely to include:

- A growth in the number of ways that potential research participants can be contacted, with the focus being specifically mobile, for example more mobile panels and new river sampling options*.
- More use of in-the-moment research, which means shifting the balance from administered research to participant research.
- More location-based approaches, such as geofencing, geo-tracking, and geo-tagging.
- Greater use of passive data collection.
- More integration of mobile data into a broader big data framework.

* River sampling refers to samples that are created dynamically from online populations using methods such as banners and online promotions (Oliver 2011).

Researchers need to be aware of the opportunities being created by the changes taking place in and around the mobile ecosystem, but they also need to be aware of the need to conduct empirical research into the consequences of the changes. Mobile research holds out the prospect of reaching people who may have been harder to reach through other means and the opportunity to reach people in new and varied situations. However, the impact on the data in terms of sample frame differences and mode effects need to be carefully assessed and measured.

References

Baker, R. (2011, August 8). The mobile hype ends here. *Research-Live*. Retrieved from http://www.research-live.com/comment/the-mobile-hype-ends-here/4005776.article

Blumberg, J. & **Luke, J.** (2014, July). *Wireless Substitution: Early Release of Estimates From the. National Health Interview Survey, July–December 2013.* CDC. Retrieved from http://www.cdc.gov/nchs/data/nhis/earlyrelease/wireless201407.pdf

Chadwick, S. (2014, July). It's the year of the mobile. Again. *Research World*.

Downes-Le Guin, T., Baker, R., Mechling, J., & **Ruyle, E.** (2012). Myths and realities of respondent engagement in online surveys. *International Journal of Market Research, 54*(5). DOI: http://dx.doi.org/10.2501/IJMR-54-5-613-633

ESOMAR. (2014). *Global Market Research,*

GRIT. (2014). *GreenBook Research Industry Trends Report,* Fall 2014. Retrieved from https://www.greenbook.org/grit/2014

Oliver, L. (2011, November). *River Sampling Non probability sampling in an online environment,* Retrieved from http://lexolivier.blogspot.co.uk/2011/11/river-sampling-non-probability-sampling.html

Peterson, G. (2012). *Unintended mobile respondents.* Annual Council of American Survey Research Organizations Technology Conference, New York, USA.

Poynter, R. (2014, January 27). *Stop asking when mobile will be the next big thing, it happened a year or two ago!.* NewMR Blog, Retrieved from http://newmr.org/stop-asking-when-mobile-will-be-the-next-big-thing-it-happened-a-year-or-two-ago/

Poynter, R., Williams, N., & **York, S.** (2014). The Handbook of Mobile Market Research. Wiley.

Revilla, M., Toninelli, D., Ochoa, C., & **Loew, G.** (2014, October). *Do online access panels really need to allow and adapt surveys to mobile devices?.* RECSM Working Paper Number 41. Retrieved from http://www.upf.edu/survey/_pdf/RECSM_wp041.pdf

CHAPTER 3

Using Mobile Phones for High-Frequency Data Collection

Amparo Ballivian*, João Pedro Azevedo* and
Will Durbin*

*World Bank, aballivian@worldbank.org,
jazevedo@worldbank.org, sdurbin@worldbank.org

Abstract

The 'Listening to Latin America and the Caribbean' ('Listening to LAC' or 'L2L') project was motivated by the financial crisis of 2008, when policy makers in the region asked the World Bank how the crisis would affect their efforts to reduce poverty and what policy responses they could design to mitigate those impacts. Unfortunately, little data existed to answer this question, as poverty data is collected infrequently. The L2L project aimed to answer this key question: Can we use cellular phone communication technology to reduce the time and cost of collecting household survey data from a probabilistic sample without compromising data quality? This paper presents the results of two pilots of this mode of data collection in Peru and Honduras that allowed us to test this question empirically. The results suggest that using mobile phones for short and frequent surveys can produce high-quality data more quickly – and more cheaply on a per survey basis – than traditional methods, and can be a valuable complement to less frequent, more comprehensive, more expensive household surveys. But, in order for mobile data to produce timely information for policy decisions, the system for mobile surveys must be in place before the crisis starts. In other words, the L2L model cannot be launched after the onset of a crisis. This is because: (i) in order to ensure statistical representativeness, an appropriate sample must be drawn; (ii) it takes some time to recruit the panel; and (iii) an initial face-to-face interview is needed to collect data on

How to cite this book chapter:
Ballivian, A, Azevedo, J P, and Durbin, W. 2015. Using Mobile Phones for High-Frequency Data Collection. In: Toninelli, D, Pinter, R & de Pedraza, P (eds.) *Mobile Research Methods: Opportunities and Challenges of Mobile Research Methodologies*, Pp. 21–39. London: Ubiquity Press. DOI: http://dx.doi.org/10.5334/bar.c. License: CC-BY 4.0.

the socio-economic characteristics of each household, which cannot be done by mobile phones due to the large number of questions. In addition, several implementation issues explained in this report need to be addressed ahead of time. For this reason it is not possible to initiate the program of data collection immediately after the onset of a crisis and obtain relevant data quickly. Therefore, the most desirable use of the L2L model of mobile surveys may be as a complement to on-going national surveys which collect mobile phone numbers of household members.

Keywords

poverty, household surveys, mobile data, panel surveys, data quality, SMS, CATI, IVR

Listening to Latin America and the Caribbean ('Listening to LAC')

Background

Evidence-based decision making for poverty alleviation has evolved considerably in the past 30 years. Whereas in the 1980s only 25 countries had regular household surveys, today the World Bank's external microdata catalog has 1,580 household surveys on 183 countries. But the data collection mechanisms used today are virtually the same as those used since probabilistic survey data started being collected: after the sample is drawn, a number of interviewers travel to peoples' homes, they ask the household head dozens of questions verbally, they record the answers on a paper form and, several weeks or months later, the answers are transferred to a digital support. Only then can data analysis begin. All this is costly, takes a long time and is prone to error. Recent advances in survey data collection are introducing digital technology to replace paper questionnaires, thereby reducing time and errors in data transcription. But the time and cost involved in traveling to respondents' living locations remain essentially the same.

Reducing the time to collect data, particularly in crisis situations, may make the difference between adopting policy actions based on evidence or on guesses. Regardless of the nature of the crisis – economic, political, social, natural disasters or other – policy makers and public authorities need to address these situations within days, or at most weeks, after the onset of the crisis. When these crises happen in developing countries, donors that provide financial or technical assistance also find themselves bound by these very narrow timeframes. Traditional data collection methods simply do not produce data and corresponding analyses quickly enough to be used as evidence supporting short-term policy decisions. Cost considerations are also important drivers of survey frequency, so reducing cost can also lead to more frequent data collection.

In parallel, information and communication technologies, and in particular the signal coverage and rate of use of cellular phones, has expanded exponentially in developing countries. The 'Listening to Latin America and the Caribbean' ('Listening to LAC' or 'L2L') pilot attempted to take advantage of these two trends – an increasingly ubiquitous modern technology and a rise in evidence-based policy making – to produce more frequent data for policy decisions following crises situations. The key question that the L2L project aimed to answer is this: *Can we use cell phone communication technology to reduce the time and cost of collecting probabilistic sample data without compromising data quality?* [6]

Telephone interviewing has three main problems: (1) obtaining representative samples of the national population; (2) obtaining adequate response rates; and (3) data quality compared to face-to-face interviewing, which is the standard method of survey data collection in developing countries. The L2L pilot tested for the prevalence and seriousness of these problems in a systematic way.

The L2L pilot showed that it is possible to conduct nationally representative surveys using cell phones provided that an adequate sampling frame is used. To examine data quality issues, the L2L pilot attempted to answer some subsidiary questions, such as: (1) Do different cell phone technologies (SMS, IVR, CATI)[7] have different attrition rates (L2L used a panel of respondents; attrition refers to the drop-out rate over panel waves)? (2) What is the quality of the data collected, in terms of external validity (comparison with traditional methods), internal validity (internal consistency of answers) and reliability (consistency of answers over time/methods)? (3) Do attrition rates differ between countries (Peru and Honduras)? (4) Do attrition rates vary according to observable characteristics, such as age, gender and the education level of the head of household? (5) Does offering an incentive affect attrition rates? Do incentives affect attrition rates differently across different groups and is the impact of incentives country-dependent? (6) What are the costs of the different methods of cell phone communication for eliciting survey responses?

---

[6] The use of cellular phones for data collection commonly involves using crowd-sourcing, but this method is not viable when analysis needs a statistically valid, representative sample that allows researchers to make statistical inferences about the population. Crowd-sourced surveys suffer from selection bias. For this reason, while they are extremely valuable in some situations, they are often not an effective tool for making policy decisions concerning the population at large.

[7] SMS is the well-known acronym for Short Message Service, which allows communications between two mobile phones using short messages (maximum 160 characters). IVR is a lesser known acronym for Interactive Voice Recognition, an audio message sent over telephone lines by a computer application. CATI is the acronym for Computer-Assisted Telephone Interview, in which a person interviews another by voice communication using a telephone. The last two can be used with landline or mobile telephones.

This summary paper presents the results of two pilots of this mode of data collection in two developing countries, Peru and Honduras, and the analysis of the characteristics of the resulting response rates and data quality attributes.

Project concept and design

The pilots were designed to test the response rates and the quality of data, while also providing some information on the cost of collecting data using mobile phones. Moreover, while mobile phone surveys may produce high-quality data for some types of survey questions, such as those typically asked in marketing research, it was important to test whether the method would work as well with survey questions aimed at eliciting information on poverty and vulnerability, which are typically more sensitive.

Because traditionally poverty rates are calculated at the household level, we decided to interview households instead of individuals. Another reason to study households and not individuals is that, unlike in a face-to-face interview, in a mobile phone survey it may be very difficult (indeed, impossible in some situations) to know precisely who is answering the questionnaire.[8]

Because we did not know the distribution of phone ownership, coverage or actual use per socio-economic characteristics, to minimize bias we did not sample from telephone records. Instead, we used two different nationally representative sampling frameworks: the official one provided by the national statistical agency in Peru and the Gallup World Poll sampling framework in Honduras.[9]

We started with an in-person visit to households, following traditional sampling techniques. During this initial face-to-face interview, we gathered baseline information on household characteristics and recruited participants. Since we adopted a panel design in order to test data quality issues in tracking welfare over time, we also used this initial survey to recruit the panel. Interviews were only conducted with households who gave expressed consent to do so. During the face to face interview, households also were asked about their willingness to participate in the follow up surveys via cell phone. Those who accepted signed a written consent form.

We were particularly interested in studying the welfare impacts of a potential crisis in two segments of the population: (i) the vulnerable population, loosely

---

[8] For each mobile phone survey, we attempted to ensure that the respondent was a member of the household by asking two validation questions (year of birth and gender) to match the answers with the household roster obtained at the initial face-to-face interview. We have not reviewed this data yet, but the initial results are not very encouraging, in the sense that there appears to be a significant amount of discrepancy between the household roster and the data provided in the mobile survey for year of birth and gender of the respondent.

[9] Through a competitive bidding process, Gallup won the contract to implement L2L on the ground.

defined as those households that may fall into poverty following a negative shock (e.g., a financial or food-price crisis); and (ii) the upwardly-mobile, loosely defined as that segment of the population that may escape poverty following a positive shock (e.g., a boom in commodity prices). This affected sampling choices.

We also wanted to explore the impact of incentives on the minimization of panel attrition. For this purpose, we randomly assigned households to three groups: one third of households received US$1 in free airtime for each questionnaire they answered, one third received US$5 in free airtime and one third (the control group) received no financial incentive.

In summary, the design of the projects mixed some elements of traditional surveys, such as probabilistic sampling and an initial face-to-face interview to recruit the panel, with modern technology to collect frequent data.

A. Technological choices

The first set of decisions we confronted involved the technology to use to communicate with respondents frequently: internet or cellular phones? Text-based or audio-based? Collecting surveys through free internet programs is very common today. But internet use is still low in developing countries – on average only 32 percent of the population use internet regularly; in Honduras and Peru, the percentage is 18 and 39, respectively, in 2013. Furthermore, internet users tend to be more educated, more urban and wealthier than the population at large. And reaching a pre-defined person or household through the internet can be very challenging. In contrast, mobile phone coverage is already very high in Latin America and the Caribbean (see **Table 1**), so the first decision was to collect high-frequency data using cellular phones. [10]

In order to determine the viability of using cellular phones to collect survey data, pre-tests were carried out in Peru and Nicaragua in 2010. In each country, the World Bank team worked with ad-hoc (not probabilistic) samples of individuals in different settings (e.g., urban, semi-urban, rural) and among different demographic groups (young, old, men, women) to test the facility with which individuals were able to answer survey questions using cellular phones. These pre-tests were implemented using Episurveyor, a software application to collect survey data using internet on mobile phones. The trials suggested that the majority of individuals had little difficulty using cell phones. However, the pre-test showed that the response rates would decline substantially beyond 10 questions. The pre-test also showed that, while most people own a cellular phone in urban areas, some of the poorest households in remote areas did not own a phone. Lastly, the pre-test made it clear that familiarity with cell phone features was more common among the young, and that poor rural women were

---

[10] However, the profile of internet usage in the developing world today is in many ways similar to that of the early adopters of the mobile phone, so internet-based surveys may become an option in the near future.

	Honduras	Peru	LAC average
Mobile cellular subscriptions (per 100 people)	103*	101*	109*
Population covered by a mobile-cellular network (%)	86	97	98
Households with a mobile telephone (%)	81	73	84
Population using mobile internet (%)	2.9	5.8	4.4

Table 1: Mobile phone coverage in Honduras, Peru, and LAC average, 2010.
  * 2011 data.
Source: World Bank, *Information and Communications for Development 2012: Maximizing Mobile;* www.worldbank.org/ict/IC4D2012.

particularly difficult to reach (though not necessarily because the interviewers were using mobile phones).[11] These factors pointed to the use of communication technologies that can work using the simplest possible mobile phone and the cellular technology networks that have the largest coverage.

When choosing a mode of data collection, we considered a variety of factors. One was coverage of the target population. Another practical consideration was cost. The characteristics of the different modes of communicating between enumerators and respondents and some of the advantages and disadvantages of these modes for the purpose of collecting survey data are summarized in **Table 2**.

While internet surveys and mobile survey apps offer many advantages, they can be used only on smartphones, which are concentrated among the wealthy in urban areas. In addition, indicators of overall mobile phone coverage rates can be misleading because, while the *overall* geographic coverage of cellular communications is increasing, the coverage of communication networks used by smartphones (internet on cellular networks) is still very limited in developing countries. So, mobile phone survey programs based on mobile internet technology would probably be biased against the poor and vulnerable, precisely the subjects of policy attention in times of crises. In addition, we learned during the project design phase that USSD is not usually marketed in Latin America, since the regulations for its use have not been approved.

Consequently, the surveys in both Peru and Honduras used the three remaining communication technologies – SMS, IVR and CATI – but the survey designs (sample segmentation and contact frequency) were deliberately different. In Peru, households were randomly assigned to a communication mode (SMS, IVR, CATI), which stayed constant for all rounds, or waves, of the survey. In Honduras, all the survivor group of households (the households that

---

[11] This difficulty was encountered by our pre-test interviewer (white, American, male) but we simply intend to report it and not draw conclusions. For more information on the effects on responses of the gender, tribe and religion matches of the enumerator and the respondent see Baird et al. (2008).

	Audio/ Text	Self-Administered (Yes/No)	Pros	Cons
SMS **(Short Message Service)**	Text	Yes	Low cost	Maximum 160 characters Requires literacy Does not allow visual aids Automated
IVR **(Interactive Voice Recognition)**	Audio	Yes	No need for interviewers	Often viewed as annoying Medium cost Does not allow visual aids
CATI **(Computer-Assisted Telephone Interview)**	Audio	No	Respondent can ask to clarify questions	Higher cost than SMS or IVR, mainly because: (i) voice is more expensive than text communications; and (ii) operators' salaries need to be paid Does not allow visual aids
USSD **(Unstructured Supplementary Services Data)**	Text	Yes	No length limitations	Requires close collaboration and approval by telecom companies Not commonly marketed in LAC region Does not allow visual aids
Mobile internet	Text	Yes	No length limitations Lower cost than voice communications Allows use of visual aids	Limited mobile internet coverage in LAC region Requires smartphones

Table 2: Pros and cons of mobile technologies for survey data collection.

responded to the first questionnaire) was exposed to all three communication modes. Both designs allow for validity tests, while only the Honduran design allowed for reliability tests.[12] The Honduran design was a test-retest design of the communication mode, which is closely related to the difference-in-difference methodology of experimental evaluation. Importantly, the questionnaires were worded exactly the same way, regardless of the mode, which meant short questions, since SMS is limited to 160 characters.

B. Incentives

In order to minimize non-response, three types of incentives were given. First, households that did not own a mobile phone were provided one for free.[13] Approximately 127 phones were donated in Honduras and 200 in Peru. Second, all communications between the interviewers and the households were free to the respondents. Finally, households were randomly assigned to one of three incentive levels – US$0, US$1 or US$5 – which were distributed after completion of each mobile survey. Unfortunately, mobile payments are not very developed in Latin America,[14] so instead of money transfers the pilot transferred the equivalent in free airtime minutes to each respondent's mobile phone account.

C. Sample design

The sample size was 1,500 households in each country, though sampling was done in different ways in Peru and in Honduras. In Peru, where the World Bank has a very close working relationship with the National Statistics Institute (Instituto Nacional de Estadística e Informática, INEI), the L2L sample was based on the sampling frame for the national household survey (Encuesta Nacional de Hogares, ENAHO) conducted by INEI every three months. In Honduras, the sampling was done deliberately without using the National Statistics Institute's sampling frame, in order to test the feasibility of replication of the L2L model in countries where a strong relationship with the statistics office is absent. Instead, the sampling frame used was the Gallup World Poll sampling frame, which is regularly conducted in 160 countries.

In Peru, the sample selection was guided by the following criteria: (i) the sample should be representative nationally, and in urban and rural areas; and (ii) households close to poverty line should be oversampled because policy decisions in time of crises need to be especially mindful of the poor and vulner-

---

[12]   We tested for reliability using Cronbach's alpha, a measure of internal consistency, that is, how closely related a set of items are as a group. A 'high' value of alpha is often used as evidence that the items measure an underlying construct. Please see www.worldbank.org/lacpoverty/l2l for further details.

[13]   A generous donation from Brightstar Corporation made this possible.

[14]   See, for instance: http://mobilereadiness.mastercard.com/the-index

able. For the purposes of this project, 'close to poverty line' was defined as the 40 percent of consumption distribution that symmetrically bands the national poverty line: 20 percent above and 20 percent below. In 27 percent of Peruvian households monthly per capita consumption was below the moderate poverty line in 2010 (ENAHO). Consequently, households whose monthly per capita consumption fell between 7 and 47 percent of the national distribution were oversampled.

Honduras did not have an income oversample because the poverty rate is 60 percent, so oversampling 20 percent above the poverty rate would include a large portion of the middle class, which is likely not the most vulnerable in times of crisis. Furthermore, in countries with high poverty rates the poverty line would likely be very close to the average income, so the income distribution would already include a large percentage both of the vulnerable (just above the poverty line) and of households below but close to the poverty line (who may escape poverty in case of positive shocks).

D. Questionnaire design[15]

For the initial face-to-face surveys the starting point was the official national household survey questionnaire. Step-wise regressions were done to select the set of questions that best predicted consumption. For the purposes of robustness, the regressions were also done with questions that best predicted income, which yielded the same results. A similar procedure was done in Honduras, except that only best predictors of income were chosen, because Honduras did not have a recent consumption aggregate. For the monthly cell phone surveys the pre-test results and other mobile surveys done elsewhere revealed that attrition and non-response increase significantly with the number of questions, and especially after 10 questions. So a maximum of 10 questions had to be chosen for the monthly questionnaire.

Most questions were time-variant and each questionnaire was repeated to observe if answers changed over time. All questions related to variables that strongly affect household welfare and that are likely to change in times of crisis. To simplify the questionnaire and avoid 'recency' effects[16] in the CATI and IVR modes, only questions admitting yes/no answers were chosen. In addition, one set of questions was the food security module developed by the U.S. Department of Agriculture specifically to test the internal validity of the responses using Rasch analysis.

---

[15] Please see www.worldbank.org/lacpoverty/l2l for copies of the questionnaires and related materials.

[16] Recency is the tendency for respondents to answer the last option in a list of possible answers due to low memory retention. Recency is more common in audio modes of survey deployment. See Krosnick and Alwin (1987).

E. Costs

The implementation of both face-to-face and mobile phone surveys also provided actual cost data for implementing each method. The implementing agency, Gallup, provided this information on the basis of actual costs incurred, as summarized in **Table 3**.

Pilot results

There was no intention of the pilot to make inferences about the Peruvian or Honduran populations in terms of welfare, education, health or other questions asked, based on the answers to the L2L survey questions.[17] Rather, we analyzed the results of the different data collection modes along two lines: (i) attrition rates and the behavior of these rates in relation to household characteristics, survey mode and incentive level; and (ii) data quality.

Peru

Two thirds of recruited households in Peru failed to answer the first round of follow-up surveys. As **Table 4** shows, attrition slightly increased with each wave of the survey (between 1 and 3 percentage points per wave), reaching 75 percent in wave 6.

Regarding the mode of communication with respondents in Peru, higher attrition rate and lower survey completion rate was found among panelists who were exposed to self-administered modes (IVR and SMS), as **Table 5** shows. Over the course of the six waves the level of attrition for SMS increased to 79 percent (initial face-to-face compared with wave 6) and to 61 percent for CATI, with attrition for IVR remaining stable (81 percent). It should be noted that the L2L project deliberately sent out more invitations to take part via SMS (n = 677), compared to IVR (n = 383) and CATI (n = 384). Since the level of attrition for SMS is relatively high compared to the CATI group, the higher n-size of the SMS group drives up the overall attrition of the panel.

Moreover, IVR and SMS have the disadvantage of a large proportion of respondents only answering some of the questions in any given survey, meaning that respondents completely skipped some questions.[18] IVR and SMS are both self-administered methods, while CATI relies on an interviewer whose job it is to ensure all questions are read, understood and answered by the respondents (recording even legitimate 'Don't Know' responses or 'Refusals').

---

[17] Although there is nothing wrong with doing these inferences, given the probabilistic nature of the sample, and we hope other researchers will do so.

[18] Giving a 'don't know' answer or refusing to answer a question is not considered as a skip. If a respondent skips a question no data were obtained at all.

Methodology	Cost Per Interview	Cost Per Year (12 monthly surveys)
Face-to-face	40	720,000
CATI	25	450,000
IVR	17	306,000
SMS	8	144,000

Table 3: Costs for a sample of 1,500 surveys (in US dollars).

Wave 1	Wave 2	Wave 3	Wave 4	Wave 5	Wave 6
67%	68%	69%	70%	72%	75%

Table 4: Overall attrition rates in successive waves, Peru.

	IVR	SMS	CATI
Wave 1	80%	70%	49%
Wave 2	75%	75%	47%
Wave 3	78%	76%	49%
Wave 4	78%	75%	52%
Wave 5	84%	76%	53%
Wave 6	81%	79%	61%

Table 5: Attrition by Methodology in Peru.

Among Peruvian panelists surveyed about why they did not respond (after the completion of the six waves in the panel survey), 26 percent said they would prefer to be interviewed by a person. Also, panelists responding to the surveys via IVR or SMS showed a higher propensity to leave questions unanswered than did respondents answering via CATI. In short, interviewers were important for getting higher response rates and ensuring that respondents gave consideration to all the survey questions.

Economic incentives in the form of mobile phone credit for every completed survey did not seem to have a big effect on the post-recruitment response rate in Peru (see **Table 6**). However, as the panel exercise progressed, incentives seemed to have had some effect on minimizing attrition. It should be noted that a considerably higher incentive (5 dollars) did not prove much more successful in reducing attrition than a smaller amount (1 dollar).

	No incentive	1 USD	5 USD
Wave 1	**68%**	**66%**	**66%**
Wave 2	70%	67%	66%
Wave 3	73%	68%	68%
Wave 4	72%	70%	67%
Wave 5	76%	71%	69%
Wave 6	**80%**	**73%**	**71%**

Table 6: Attrition by Incentive Level in Peru.

Honduras

The initial attrition rate – that is, the proportion of respondents who agreed to participate in the panel after the initial face-to-face survey but did not answer the first round of surveys – was considerably lower in Honduras than in Peru in the three survey modes. The final attrition rate was also lower in Honduras, across all survey modes. As in Peru, CATI surveys generated the lowest attrition, but the difference was more pronounced in the case of Honduras (see **tables 7** and **8**).

While in Peru 67 percent of recruited households failed to answer the first round of follow-up surveys, in Honduras this percentage was only 41. However, the gap between the initial and final attrition – that is, the additional number of panelists that dropped out of the panel between the first follow-up survey and the end of the study – was similar in both countries: in Peru the final attrition was eight percentage points higher than the initial attrition rate and in Honduras it was nine percentage points higher than the initial attrition rate.

In contrast to Peru, economic incentives in the form of mobile phone credit did have a considerable effect on post-recruitment response rate in Honduras. Also in contrast to Peru, the size of the incentive mattered in the Honduran study, with higher incentives being more effective in minimizing attrition (see **Table 9**). It is worth noting that Honduran panelists had to work harder

Initial F2F to Wave 1 (Peru)/ Week 1 (Honduras)	Peru	Honduras
IVR	80%	60%
SMS	70%	55%
CATI	49%	12%
Overall	**67%**	**41%**

Table 7: Initial Attrition/Non-Response by Methodology (Peru vs. Honduras).

Initial F2F to End of Panel Study	Peru	Honduras
IVR	81%	62%
SMS	79%	60%
CATI	61%	28%
Overall	75%	50%

Table 8: Final Attrition/Non-Response by Methodology (Peru vs. Honduras).

No incentive		1 USD	5 USD
From F2F to Wave 1	45%	41%	38%
F2F to end of panel	54%	52%	43%

Table 9: Attrition by Incentive Level in Honduras.

than their Peruvian counterparts: the former had to answer up to three surveys per month, while the latter only answered one survey per month.

Characteristics of non-respondents and the attrite

Higher attrition rates were found among older, less educated, less affluent panelists and among households living in rural areas in both countries. The mobile panel's high attrition among these types of respondents does not necessarily invalidate it as a viable method for nationally representative studies. As long as the attrite population is not systematically different from the respondent population, parameter estimates will not be biased, but their variance will increase as a result of a smaller sample size. This effect can be effectively addressed by increasing the panel size and applying a post-stratification (weighting) scheme.[19]

Data quality tests

Research aimed to answer two questions related to data quality, validity and reliability:

Question 1: Can the SMS method yield valid measurements, i.e. measurements that are comparable, within an acceptable margin of error,

---

[19] For details on weighting schemes, please refer to 'Baseline face-to-face Surveys in Honduras and Peru. Methodological Report' by Gallup. For additional information on the characteristics of the attrite population please refer to the full report.

to those produced by face-to-face interviews, which is the benchmark standard for surveys?

Question 2: Are estimates generated by SMS statistically reliable (that is, stable or consistent across repeated iterations of the same SMS measurement)?[20]

To answer the first question the team applied a criterion validity test, i.e. a comparative analysis between a test and a criterion variable that is supposed to measure the same construct and that is held to be valid. The L2L face-to-face survey was adopted as the criterion measurement for the analyses. Since the SMS sample was affected by a high level of attrition only households that responded to both surveys (45% of the sample) were included in the analysis, in order to ensure that whatever differences might be encountered between the two measures could primarily be attributed to 'mode effects', as opposed to demographic differences between respondents. The difference between the responses given to the test variable and those given to the criterion variable were tested for statistical significance by means of non-parametric analysis of variance (ANOVA).

The results generated by SMS and face-to-face surveys were compared for eight different questions. These questions inquired about factual information on household infrastructure (i.e. possession of TV, type of sanitation facilities, etc.), factual information on access to the internet inside or outside the household, and perceptual information (i.e. whether the respondents considered themselves poor). The responses to all questions by SMS differed from those collected via face-to-face by at least 7.4 percentage points, a margin that is statistically significant at the 95% confidence level. Interestingly, responses given via SMS indicate lower availability of water/sanitation and television ownership, but almost twice as much access to the internet compared to face-to-face responses. In addition, the self-perception of poverty was higher when asked via SMS than face-to-face.

Similar criterion validity tests were performed for IVR and CATI. The responses collected via IVR show a similar pattern as those collected via SMS, with items related to household infrastructure receiving lower 'yes' scores when asked via IVR compared to face-to-face, while the items related to 'internet access' and 'self-perceptions on poverty' received higher scores. As in the case of SMS, the observed differences between IVR and face-to-face are statistically significant. The answers collected via CATI, on the other hand, were almost identical to the ones collected face-to-face, with no item showing a statistically significant difference. Since the same panelists responding to the IVR and CATI surveys also responded to SMS surveys, the differences in responses observed

---

[20]   These questions were analyzed only for the Honduras pilot. The numerical results of the validity and reliability tests are available in the full report online, as well as additional multivariate analysis of attrition.

between SMS, CATI and IVR, or between any of these and face-to-face cannot be attributed to demographic differences between them.

Regarding the second data quality question, in order to test the reliability of measurements two identical measurements were performed of the same questions analyzed in the criterion validity analysis discussed above. Gallup performed repeated administrations of these questions by means of face-to-face, IVR and CATI on the same group of panelists in Honduras only. In all cases, the repeated measurements were performed within a minimum of 10 weeks from the first administration.

The results indicate that the SMS surveys performed quite satisfactorily in terms of generating reliable measurements. This conclusion is supported by the fact that Cronbach's Alpha reliability coefficient obtained for SMS (0.74) is very close to the one obtained for face-to-face (0.77) in the same test-retest exercise. Also, as can be expected, the items inquiring about factual information (i.e. on household infrastructure) show a higher reliability than the items measuring perceptions of poverty.

IVR stands out as the method that generated the most reliable responses overall, followed by SMS and CATI which came quite close to each other. Interestingly, IVR responses proved very reliable for all the items tested, outperforming the other two methods in all but one item ('past-30-day access to the Internet), where CATI fared somewhat better. However, while IVR was more reliable, its advantage was relatively small.

It is also interesting that both IVR and CATI outperformed SMS in those items that inquire about personal internet access, a result that could be explained by the pattern observed in the criterion validity analysis, where SMS surveys were most often responded to by younger informants. Therefore, it would appear that the reliability of these questions tends to be affected by an 'informant switching' behavior when asked via SMS.

The CATI responses show an intriguing pattern: both perceptual and factual items behaved somewhat unreliably when compared to the internet-related items for the same method. It should be remembered that CATI was the best-performing method in terms of criterion validity, with almost identical responses to the ones collected via face-to-face.

Another important aspect of this analysis is the fact that the self-administered vs. interviewer-administered dimension does not seem to explain the reliability differences encountered. The top performing method (IVR) is a self-administered method, while SMS and CATI – which fared similarly in the test – are self-administered and interviewer-administered methods, respectively. It should be remembered that the presence of interviewers (or their absence) was a crucial factor in explaining the differences found in the criterion validity analysis. So, since it is no longer the case for the reliability analysis, alternative explanations need to be considered.

A closer look at the survey methods being evaluated suggests that IVR was probably the one that required the shortest time and was least prone to human error (on the interviewer side). The IVR system would call respondents and play a pre-recorded greeting, followed by instructions and the actual survey questions. Respondents had to press buttons on their mobile phone keypads to answer the questions. The use of a recording guaranteed that the questions were read exactly the same way in each administration, thus controlling for potential errors derived from inconsistent question reading. Besides, it is possible that respondents had to pay close attention to these recordings, as it was obvious that they would not be able to obtain much help or clarification if they missed something.

SMS, on the other hand, relies on the respondent's reading comprehension ability and attention span. Since questions remain in the phone's inbox until the respondent answers them, respondents could conceivably multitask during the survey administration without missing questions. Somewhat similarly, the CATI surveys could have been affected by human factors. Due to logistic considerations, the interviewers who conducted the first surveys were not necessarily the same ones that conducted the second administrations. Thus, although unlikely, there could have been significant variance in speed of reading, intonation, clarity, mastery of the questionnaire, etc.

Alternatively, it could be hypothesized that having a different interviewer re-contact the households to ask the exact same questions could have brought back some anxiety or fear in some respondents. If such was the case, the findings would suggest that, for panel studies such as this one, having no human contact in the administration of repeat surveys is more beneficial for reliability purposes than having inconsistent human contact. This remains, nonetheless, an intriguing set of findings that would require additional research to be understood in a more satisfactory manner.

Importantly, for all methodologies the 'yes' responses were quite consistent, which means most of the variability observed was due to inconsistencies between the 'No' and 'Don't know/Refused' answers. This is an aspect that deserves proper attention as it demonstrates that no methodology performed poorly in terms of consistently accounting for 'presence' of the phenomena inquired.

Conclusions

The pilots showed that it is possible to do mobile surveys from a nationally representative panel of respondents, but that attrition rates are relatively high and country-specific. Economic incentives can be used to contain attrition, but they work better over repeated waves of the panel.

Data quality tests of validity of the data (for Honduras surveys) showed that answers to SMS and IVR modes were statistically significantly different from answers to the same questions in face-to-face interviews. Responses in the CATI method, on the other hand, were virtually the same as those in face-to-face interviews. In terms of data reliability tests all methods performed well, with IVR showing the highest reliability.

When choosing between voice and text interviewing, the advantage of text was lower cost; the advantage of CATI was substantially lower attrition rates. A combination of both voice and text is suggested to be explored in future research, in the same spirit as the recent trend of combined landline and mobile phone surveys in the United States.

IVR does not have any advantages over SMS, either in terms of cost or response rates. IVR has the additional inconvenience that survey calls are lost for good when not answered immediately (as opposed to SMS surveys where messages remain in the phone's inbox allowing for a later response). While IVR responses did prove the most reliable data in the test-retest, the small differences in terms of reliability with the other modes suggest that IVR is not a very suitable mode to communicate with respondents (at least for these types of surveys).

Finally, mobile phone surveys have certain practical disadvantages vis-à-vis face-to-face interviews, such as unstable coverage of mobile networks and sometimes lack of electricity to re-charge phones. On the other hand, mobile phone surveys overcome security problems in regions that are prone to conflicts or natural disasters, so they may be a good option in fragile environments.

We are hopeful that disclosing the L2L data to the public will encourage researchers to conduct further analyses. As mobile phone penetration continues to expand in developing countries, we expect this to become an accepted method for collecting survey data more frequently, and hope that this leads to more evidence-based policy decisions when governments and donors are confronted with sudden shocks.

Acknowledgements

This paper is a summary of a larger report on the project conducted by the Poverty, Equity and Gender Team of the World Bank's Latin America and Caribbean region. The project was led by Amparo Ballivian and João Pedro Azevedo and managed by Will Durbin. Additional team members included Jesus Rios, Johanna Godoy, Christina Borisova and Sabine Mireille Ntsama. This study is part of a larger effort by the World Bank to provide open access to its research and make a contribution to development policy discussions around the world. The full report, alongside with separate technical reports, the dataset, questionnaires, open source software, manuals and other materials produced under this project can be found at worldbank.org/lacpoverty/l2l. The authors encourage further research using these data and materials. The team is grateful to the following individuals who provided excellent comments: Robert Tortola, John Newman, Gabriel Demombynes, Katheleen Beegle and William Jack, as well as to the anonymous peer reviewers selected by the editor of this book. The team is also grateful to the World Bank trust funds (SFLAC, RSR and ESSD) which provided financial support, and to the Brightstar Corporation, which donated 1,000 mobile phones.

References

Alderman, H., Behrman, J.R., Kohler, H., Maluccio, J.A., & Watkins, S.C. (2001). Attrition in Longitudinal Household Survey Data. *Demographic Research, 5*(4), 79–124. DOI: http://dx.doi.org/10.4054/DemRes.2001.5.4

Baird, S., Hamory, J., & Miguel, E. (2008). *Tracking, Attrition and Data Quality in the Kenyan Life Panel Survey Round 1 (KLPS-1)*, (Center for International and Development Economics Research Working Paper). Berkeley: University of California, Berkeley. Retrieved July 29, 2015 from http://www.escholarship.org/uc/item/3cw7p1hx

Croke, K., Dabalen, A., Demombynes, G., Giugale, M., & Hoogeveen, J. (2012). *Collecting high frequency panel data using mobile phones. Does timely data lead to accountability?* (World Bank Policy Research Working Paper No. 6097). Retrieved July 29, 2015 from http://papers.ssrn.com/sol3/papers.cfm?abstract_id=2087971

Curtin, R., Presser, S., & Singer, E. (2005). Changes in Telephone Survey Nonresponse over the Past Quarter Century. *Oxford Journals/Social Sciences Public Opinion Quarterly, 69*(1), 87–98. DOI: http://dx.doi.org/10.1093/poq/nfi002

de Leeuw, E. D. (2005). To Mix or Not to Mix Data Collection Modes in Surveys. *The Journal of Official Statistics, 21*(2), 233–255.

Dillman, D. A., Phelps, G., Tortora, R. D., Swift, K., Kohrell, J., Berck, J., Messer, B. L. (2009). Response rate and measurement differences in mixed-mode surveys using mail, telephone, interactive voice response (IVR) and the Internet. *Social Science Research, 38*(1), 1–18. DOI: http://dx.doi.org/10.1016/j.ssresearch.2008.03.007

Dillon, B. (2010). *Using Mobile Phones to Conduct Research in Developing Countries.* (Cornell University Working Paper). Retrieved July 29, 2015 from http://www.edi-africa.com/docs/Dillon_MobilePhoneSurveys.pdf

Gallup. (2012). *The World Bank Listening to LAC (L2L) Pilot – Final Report.* Retrieved July 29, 2015 from http://siteresources.worldbank.org/INTLACREGTOPPOVANA/Resources/840442-1355332251652/8976232-1355959000860/Gallup-Final-Report-Oct-2012-L2L.pdf

Gallup. (2012). *The World Bank Listening to LAC (L2L) Pilot Project: Sample Design for Honduras.* Retrieved July 29, 2015 from http://siteresources.worldbank.org/INTLACREGTOPPOVANA/Resources/840442-1355332251652/8976232-1355959000860/Gallup-Honduras-Sample-Specifications-L2L.pdf

Gallup. (2012). *The World Bank Listening to LAC (L2L) Pilot Project: Sample Design for Peru.* Retrieved July 29, 2015 from http://siteresources. worldbank.org/INTLACREGTOPPOVANA/Resources/840442-1355332251652/8976232-1355959000860/Gallup-Peru-Sample-Specifications-L2L.pdf

Hausman, J.A. & Wise, D. (1979). Attrition Bias in Experimental and Panel Data: The Gary Income Maintenance Experiment. *Econometrica, 47*(2), 455–473.

Keeter, S., Kennedy, C., Dimock, M., Best, J., & Craighill, P. (2006). Gauging the Impact of Growing Nonresponse on Estimates from a National RDD Telephone Survey, *Oxford Journals/Social Sciences Public Opinion Quarterly 70*(5), 759–779. DOI: http://dx.doi.org/10.1093/poq/nfl035

Lesser, V., Dillman, D., Carlson, J., Lorenz, F., Mason, R., & Willits, F. (2001, August). *Quantifying the Influence of Incentives on Mail Survey Response Rates and Their Effects on Nonresponse Error.* Paper presented at Proceedings of the Annual Meeting of the American Statistical Association. Retrieved July 29, 2015 from http://www.amstat.org/sections/srms/proceedings/y2001/Proceed/00474.pdf

Lynn P., & Kaminska O. (2013). The Impact of Mobile Phones on Survey Measurement Error. *Public Opinion Quarterly 77*(2), 586–605. DOI: http://dx.doi.org/10.1093/poq/nfs046

Nord, M., & and Hopwood, H. (2007). Does Interview Mode Matter for Food Security Measurement? Telephone versus In-Person Interviews in the Current Population Survey Food Security Supplement. *Public Health Nutrition 10*(12), 1474–1480. DOI: http://dx.doi.org/10.1017/S1368980007000857

Thomas, R., & Purdon, S. (1994). Telephone methods for social surveys. *Social Research Update,* Issue 8. Surrey: Department of Sociology, University of Surrey.

CHAPTER 4

An Overview of Mobile CATI Issues in Europe

Ana Slavec* and Daniele Toninelli[†]

*University of Ljubljana, Slovenia, ana.slavec@fdv.uni-lj.si,
†University of Bergamo, Italy, daniele.toninelli@unibg.it

Abstract

With the increasing popularity of mobile phones, there is a gradual decline in the coverage rates in landline surveys and these are no longer sustainable. Our objective is to explore various issues that arise with the incorporation of mobiles phones in surveys. We aim at providing researchers with general and practical guidelines. In particular, we focus on legal and ethical issues, and we study coverage, sampling, nonresponse, measurement and adjustment issues. We found important differences in degrees of respondents' protection between different countries. However, researchers should follow some general ethical guidelines which take this into consideration. Furthermore, we used Eurobarometer data to observe differences in phone use. In some countries mobile phone-only users are prevailing, while in others most people use both mobile and landline phones. We also discuss differences in measurement and nonresponse. Finally, we recommend some weighting approaches that can take into account the differences between the introduced segments (that is mobile, landline and overlap). Despite the strong differences observed from country to country, this work aims at summarizing and integrating various research findings and recommendations that can be widely applied to enhance the quality of collected data and minimize the impact of several of the discussed issues.

Keywords

Mobile phone surveys, legal issues, coverage, nonresponse, multiple frames

How to cite this book chapter:
Slavec, A and Toninelli, D. 2015. An Overview of Mobile CATI Issues in Europe.
   In: Toninelli, D, Pinter, R & de Pedraza, P (eds.) *Mobile Research Methods: Opportunities and Challenges of Mobile Research Methodologies*, Pp. 41–62.
   London: Ubiquity Press. DOI: http://dx.doi.org/10.5334/bar.d. License: CC-BY 4.0.

Introduction

With the increasing popularity of mobile phones, landline telephone surveys are undergoing a gradual decline in coverage and response rates (Blumberg & Luke 2013). Consequently, the traditional CATI approach is no longer sustainable in most countries and survey research organizations need to incorporate mobile phones to improve coverage. As a consequence of this integration, new complexities arise and updated guidelines are needed in order to make an optimal transition to the new data collection mode. This chapter provides an overview of the main issues related to the use of mobile phone numbers in telephone surveys, focusing on coverage, sampling, nonresponse and measurement. Most of the literature deals with the US situation, whereas there are fewer resources available which refer to European countries. The aim of this work is to summarize and integrate various research findings and recommendations and provide researchers with general guidelines that can be helpful in approaching mobile phone surveys issues. Our work focuses on countries in Europe and, where possible, compares them with the US; it omits other parts of the world where the situation is probably very different. In the less developed countries CATI has meant mobile for quite a long time; in most cases only relatively rich people have landlines.

In the first part of the chapter, we take an overview of the main legal and ethical issues connected to the use of mobile phones, especially how the topic should be treated country by country, according to the different legislations and regulations. In the second part, we discuss some topics connected with coverage issues, such as territorial coverage, within-household coverage and mobile-only coverage. Based on Eurobarometer data, we study the share of mobile-only population and the overlap of mobile and landline phone. In the third section, we discuss the main differences in nonresponse between landline and mobile phones: the research suggests that they are often narrow and, contrary to expectations, there is not much indication of poorer data quality in mobile phone surveys. In addition, we will show, using Eurobarometer data, that mobile phones cannot be used as the only frame (even in countries with very high mobile coverage). Thus, in the last part of the chapter, we show how to combine landline and mobile frames to minimize the impact of several of the discussed issues.

This requires applying a dual frame sampling design and a special system of weighting. In this regard, several approaches are introduced and compared.

Legal and ethical issues

Before conducting a survey, researchers have to take into consideration various legal and ethical issues which are usually related to the country where the survey is conducted. Even though there are specific rules and the various regulations are still changing rapidly, usually some general principles have to be followed. According to Jones (2011) there are at least three topics that should be addressed by researchers: privacy and public availability, anonymity and confidentiality, and informed consent. Privacy and public availability are mostly issues of non-reactive data collection, whereas for surveys only the remaining principles are actually relevant. Anonymity law aims at protecting the identity of potential respondents, and by means of confidentiality one aims to protect data provided in the framework of a research project. In the case of surveys, anonymity means that the responses cannot be matched with information that can practically reveal the identity of the respondent (e.g. the interviewed telephone number or its corresponding address). With confidentiality we intend that information provided by a respondent cannot be revealed to third parties. Lastly, informed consent requires the research organization to clearly inform potential respondents about the use of the collected data, its treatment and the main research purposes; this means that the organization has to provide complete information to insure that the respondent makes an autonomous and voluntary decision to participate in a survey. Given these general definitions of ethical principles, substantial differences can be actually observed in their application between cultures: for example, in the US freedom of information is legally more important than the protection of personal data, whereas in European countries, especially in Germany, it is the opposite (Grünwald 2013).

The principles listed above have resulted in several different measures or laws aiming at protecting respondents and/or information collected through surveys. In particular, focusing on phone surveys (both landline and mobile), in some countries the legislation aims at limiting the burden and the intrusiveness caused by survey participation. This is mainly achieved by providing citizens with harassment laws that could limit, for example, the number of callbacks in telephone surveys. For similar purposes, in some countries there is both an ethical and a legal identification of the most appropriate time of the day to carry surveys: this issue is especially important in the US, where there is a big time gap between different parts of the country (AAPOR Cell Phone Task Force 2010, hereafter referred to as 'AAPOR 2010'). In general, in several countries a 'do-not-call register' is set by the national authority to limit the burden caused by unsolicited contacts. According to ESOMAR (2013), in Austria, Cyprus, Germany, Latvia, Lithuania, Poland, Slovakia, Slovenia and Spain, an *opt-in* list is set: only people that asked to be included in this list can be contacted for survey purposes. Nevertheless, in some European countries (e.g. the UK and Ireland), in US and in Canada, an *opt-out* model is used: people can ask to be added to a do-not-call list. Even if, in most countries, companies that make calls for marketing purposes can check an available opt-in/opt-out lists before unsolicited contacts, usually agencies are not legally required to check this list before contacting the respondents. Exceptions are Austria, Italy, Germany, the Netherlands and Poland, where for research companies it is mandatory to check these lists prior to the unsolicited contact. A consequence of these regulations is that, in case of complaints made by people on the list about unsolicited calls, some mobile phone service providers may cut services for the caller (ESOMAR 2011). Some other countries (Japan, Brazil, South Korea and Mexico) do not have regulations at all for unsolicited contacts (ESOMAR 2013).

A functionality of mobile phones that could facilitate contacting respondents is text messaging. However, we can come across restrictions or legal limits for the use of text messages in some countries: for instance, they cannot always be used in the US (see CAN-SPAM Act 2003), whereas in Austria the respect of an opt-in list is mandatory to send these messages for mobile surveys. Another restriction of a potentially useful instrument in the US affects automatic telephone dialing systems, which cannot be used without the respondent's prior consent (AAPOR 2010).

Even though we observed different degrees of respondents' protection in different countries, and some topics are not considered by the current legislation of those countries, research organizations should also follow professional codes and guidelines. In this regard, the ICC/ESOMAR International Code on Market and Social Research suggests that 'the same fundamental, ethical and professional principles of face to face, mail and online research also apply to mobile phones surveys' (ESOMAR 2011). This means that researchers should insure respect, transparency and disclosure (identification of calling party, of the research organization, the purpose of the survey, and so on); moreover, they should guarantee confidentiality, privacy protection and the voluntary nature of participation.

A crucial aspect to be taken into consideration, strictly connected with the nature of mobile surveys, is the safety of the respondent, because the respondent might be in a situation where it is not safe to take a call (e.g. driving; in some countries it is not even legal taking a call while driving). If this is a general rule, other relevant regulations might apply in different cultures, 'which may mandate a stricter standard of practice' accordingly (ESOMAR 2011). For instance, researchers should always carefully check the legally and socially accepted age at which children can respond and seek consent from parents (for further information, see ESOMAR 1999).

Mobile phone coverage

One of the most important aspects of mobile surveys is coverage rates. As mentioned in the introduction, the principal reason for introducing mobile CATI in data collection is the declining coverage of landline surveys. According to Eurobarometer data, from 2004 to 2013 the landline coverage registered a median drop of about 17 percentage points; the highest decline rates were observed in Finland (52.7) and Czech Republic (47.1), whereas France and Hungary are two exceptions where the coverage has increased by just 2.7 and as much as 81.4 percentage points, respectively (see **Table 1**). At the same time, mobile phone coverage is gradually increasing, and it is more than compensating the trend of the landline coverage, so that the general share of no-phone population is decreasing. The median mobile coverage in Europe has increased by about 13 percentage points from 2004 to 2013, with the highest growth observed in Bulgaria, (+41.0) and Serbia (+39.3) (see same **Table 1**).

	Mobile phone	Landline phone
AT	15.4	−37.6
BE	11.2	−9.7
BG	41.0	−38.3
CY	13.5	−18.7
CZ	10.2	−47.1
DE	15.6	−4.3
DK	14.2	−33.8
EE	12.6	−18.5
ES	8.5	−17.1
FI	5.5	−52.7
FR	14.7	2.7
GB	18.2	−5.0
GR	16.2	−6.7
HU	85.2	81.4
IE	14.6	−17.9
IT	8.8	−26.6
LT	13.2	−6.3
LU	19.0	−12.8
LV	11.4	−7.4
MT	21.8	−27.2
NL	11.0	−0.2
PL	1.8	−9.8
PT	20.5	−43.4
RO	5.4	−4.9
SE	39.3	−23.2
SI	1.9	−2.3
SK	7.5	−13.9
	Median 13.2	Median −17.1
	Average 14.2	Average −19.2

Table 1: Changes in coverage rate between 2004 and 2013 (percentage points) according to Eurobarometer data (European Commission 2012a, 2012b, 2012c, 2013a, 2013b, 2013c).

Although both the mobile phone and the landline coverage are very high in many European countries, in most cases each by itself is not sufficient to reach satisfactory survey coverage of the whole population. Consequently, when designing a survey, a combination of both types of phones should be used.

The spreading of the mobile phone coverage is a phenomenon that is involving most countries, not only the European ones. In the US, for example, the National Health Interview Survey (NHIS) has been observing the increasing percentage of mobile-only households since 2003. At the end of 2005 there were less than 8% of adults living in mobile-only households, and this number grew to 14.5% at the end of 2007 and to 24.5% in 2009 (Blumberg & Luke 2009). In 2013 the mobile-only rate increased to 39.4% of households (Blumberg & Luke 2013). **Table 2** (available in the Appendix) shows how the importance of the mobile-only category changed in some European countries between 2004 and 2013 (Eurobarometer 2012a, 2012b, 2012c, 2013a, 2013b, 2013c).

Before going further with our analysis, we need to define a precise classification of the main group of potential respondents according to the kind of coverage. To describe a surveyed population according to phone coverage, Brick et al. (2005; 2006) suggest to consider the following four groups of units (see **Figure 1**): the first group includes those that are only covered by landlines (landline only), the second group consists of people that own only mobile phones (mobile only), the third is made up of those who are covered by both landline and mobile phones (overlap group), and, finally, the last group comprises those who remain uncovered (no-phone population).

In **Table 3** (based on 2013 Eurobarometer data), available in the Appendix, we can clearly see that the relative size of these four groups varies a lot from country to country. We used the data in **Table 3** to draw **Figure 2**.

For landline-only coverage the highest rates are observed in Portugal (14.3%) and Croatia (13.4%); on the other hand the Czech Republic (84.3%) and Finland (85.7%) have the highest mobile-only coverage rate. If we consider the

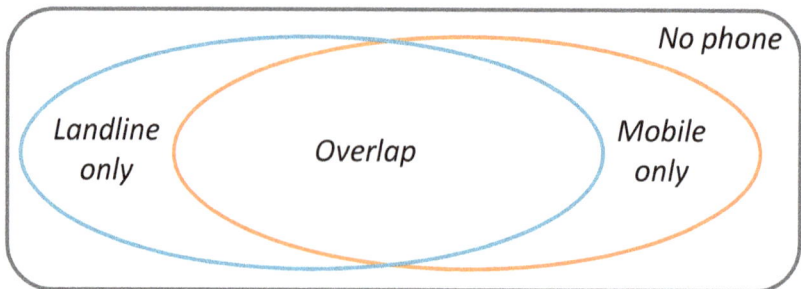

Figure 1: Four groups of phone use: mobile only, overlap, landline only, no phone.

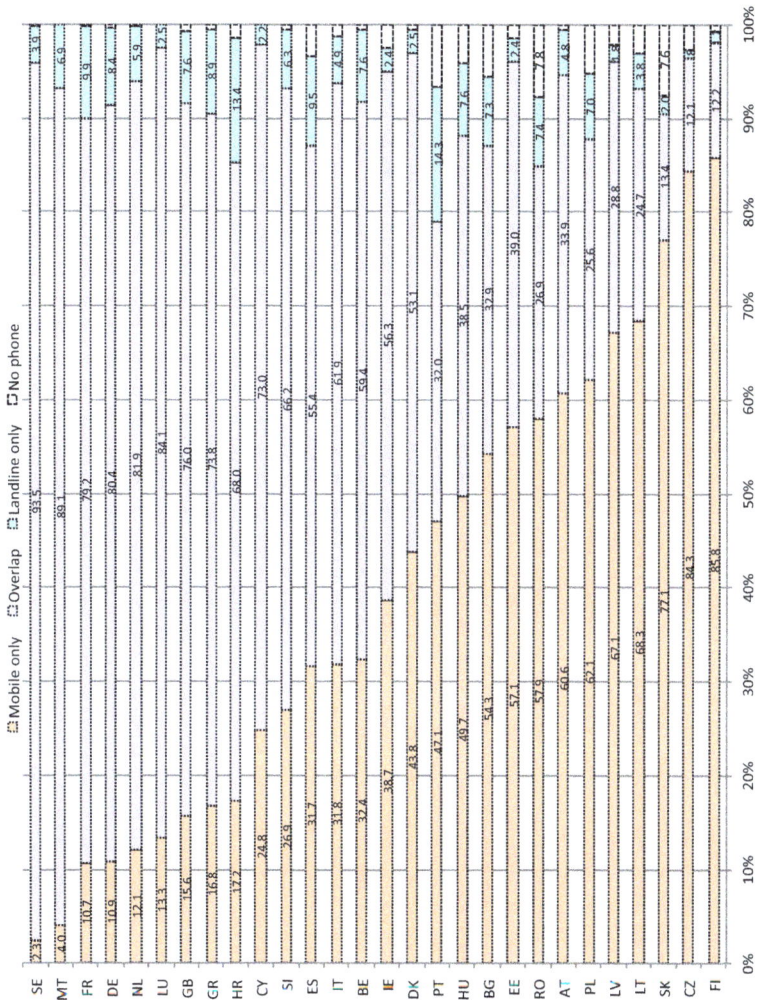

Figure 2: Phone coverage in European countries by group (European Commission 2013c).

combination of landline and mobile (overlap), the highest coverage rates are observed in Sweden (93.5%) and Malta (89.2%). For non-coverage the two highest rates are Romania (7.8%) and Slovakia (7.6%), whereas there are three countries with complete coverage: Cyprus, Malta and Luxemburg.

Even if we do not consider the noticeably high differences in coverage rates among countries, there is an additional issue that has potentially a bigger impact on the quality and representativeness of data than the coverage rate: the different groups of potential respondents have noticeably different socio-demographic characteristics. In fact, several studies showed that the mobile-only population includes mostly people who are young, well educated, with high incomes (Arthur 2007; Blumberg & Luke 2009; Fuchs 2002) and usually with more advanced technological competencies (Fuchs & Busse 2009; Nicolai 2009). On the other hand, the no-phone population is socio-demographically quite different from the mobile-only population. A question was raised by Busse and Fuchs (2012) regarding the two contradictory trends, i.e. increasing mobile-only and decreasing no-phone coverage rates: are the two effects compensating in terms of coverage bias? By studying Eurobarometer data, the two authors showed that to a certain extent there is a compensation for some variables (such as age) and in some specific countries (especially where high rates of mobile-only and of no-phone coverage is registered). Nevertheless, for other variables (such as type of community) the two effects are not being compensated, but rather they sum up; this also happens for certain countries (with high or low mobile-only and low no-phone rates).

When the population frame includes more than one territorial unit (i.e. country, region, province or municipality) and surveyed units or mobile devices cannot be precisely attributed to a specific territory, the problem of territorial coverage arises. In addition to this, sometimes, it is really hard to define the areas covered by wireless service. In fact, mobile phone service providers can have different coverage which does not necessarily overlap with landline providers; moreover, every mobile provider is likely to have a different coverage (AAPOR 2010). To make things even more complicated, it is sometimes difficult to locate a user within a country or region (e.g. there could be temporary or definitive movements of units). Moreover, a user can have more than one mobile device, and different devices can be associated with private life and/or work and used with different operators. In addition, in some countries an increased portability between operators is observed (e.g. Poggio & Callegaro 2012).

Another problem related to territory is non in-scope units; however, this is more a problem of sampling frames and will be further discussed in the next section.

A potential general solution given by the AAPOR (2010) guidelines for territorial coverage issues is simply to ask respondents for residential information during the survey. When a survey is combining landline and mobile frames, the researchers should fully disclose how the integration was dealt with within the survey.

   Finally, we will discuss within-household coverage, which can be observed when we are not sure if the answering unit corresponds to the actually selected unit. It is more common for landline phones but it can also be observed in the case of mobile phones (for instance with shared devices). In this case, we should identify the primary user of the device. However, the researcher should keep in mind that this can increase the refusal rate. Another issue is that mobile devices can also be used for business purposes. In this case, we should decide if we want to include these units, accordingly to the purpose of the survey. Usually, if we are interested in households, we include that business unit only if the device is also used for private purposes. Thus, even in the case of a business device, we should ask for additional information about the use of the device (if this is relevant to the purposes of the survey).

Sampling frames

The most important criterion for selecting a sampling frame for a survey is coverage. In the coverage section we presented Eurobarometer data (2013) which show that there are basically two groups of countries according to phone use (see **Figure 3**). First, there are countries with a very low share (less than 25%) of households that do not have a landline phone and can be reached only by a mobile phone number: the so-called 'mobile-only' population. In Europe there were nine countries with under a quarter of mobile-only population segment (from low to high): Sweden (2%), Malta (4%), France (11%), Germany (11%), the Netherlands (12%), Luxembourg (13%), the United Kingdom (16%), Croatia (17%) and Greece (17%). In these countries landline-only surveys might still be an acceptable choice if the socio-demographic differences between the segments do not produce any bias (this will be discussed in further sections). Second, in most countries the mobile-only segment is already over 25% of the population. In these countries it is necessary to also use mobile phone frames in telephone surveys. In particular, the highest percentages are observed in Finland (86%), the Czech Republic (84%) and Slovakia (77%), countries where using only the mobile frame would even be acceptable. However, for most other countries, especially Slovenia (27%) and Cyprus (25%), on the tail of this latter group, using both the mobile and the landline frame is necessary.

   'Multiple-frame surveys' refer to surveys where two or more frames are needed to cover the target population. In particular, they are used to sample rare or hard-to-reach populations, and/or populations which cannot be reached by a single frame (Groves et. al 2004). Furthermore, they usually have considerably high costs, if compared to analogously accurate single-frame designs. Dual frame samples are increasingly used in the US (see Brick et al. 2006) to address the growth of the cell-only population. However, their use in Europe is less widespread, at least to our knowledge. One of the European surveys that uses it is Flash Eurobarometer, and the sample is composed of 60% of landline and

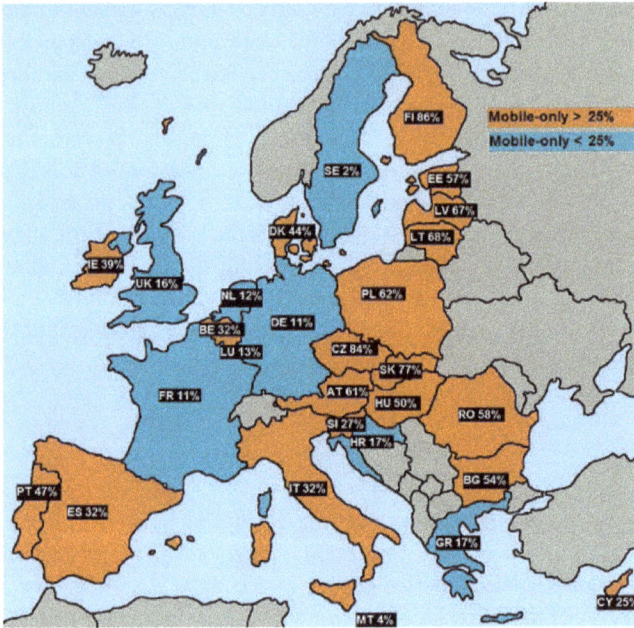

Figure 3: Mobile-only coverage in European countries.

40% of mobile numbers (European Commission 2008), where the two categories overlap. However, a study by Vehovar and Slavec (2012) showed that the
optimal composition should differ by country, according to the composition
of the four phone-use groups we defined above (mobile only, landline only,
overlap, no phone).

One of the main drawbacks of using dual frames is that people that use both
mobile and landline phones (overlap) have a higher probability of being selected
than those that use only a landline or only a mobile phone. There are two common approaches to face this issue: the screening and the weighting approach
(Brick 2009). In the screening approach, the overlap units are kept in the survey
for one frame (e.g. the mobile) and are excluded in the second frame (e.g. landline) by means of a screening question asked by the interviewer. A disadvantage
of this approach is that it is more expensive to carry out; moreover the discard-
ing of a lot of units can be viewed as a waste of resources and as an unethical
choice. The second approach, weighting (further discussed in the "Adjustment"
section), is recommended for populations for which estimates of telephone status exist. For many types of surveys, however, these estimates are not available,
and in these cases the researcher should rely on the screening approach.

The most convenient way of sampling for phone surveys is, of course, registers of telephone numbers. However, they are usually very incomplete for
mobile phones and, in some countries, even for landline phones. Thus, a

complex random digit dialing (RDD) method for sampling in telephone surveys has been developed and is commonly used for landline phone surveys in many countries. Recently, similar techniques have also been used for mobile phones; however, with different providers and many missing numbers it is even more difficult and expensive to obtain lists of phone numbers.

As previously mentioned, another sampling problem also related to territorial coverage is the presence of territorial non-in-scope units. One kind of these units is made up of users who live in a country or region different from where the mobile device was purchased. The second kind, mostly specific to North American countries, is made up of users who do not live in the same area as the exchange rate center, i.e. a geographically specified point used for determining mileage-dependent call rates: for instance, some territories do not have rate centers; subscribers can reside in a sampled territory but belong to a different rate center; some subscribers do not reside in the sampled territory but are linked to the corresponding rate center; and subscribers might have moved to a different area for a certain period of time (AAPOR 2010).

Nonresponse and measurement

In comparison to traditional landline survey methods, the newer mobile phone technologies allow the researcher to reach the potential respondent with less effort, since the mobile devices are by definition portable and the user can easily take them anywhere. In addition, many users almost constantly check their devices. As a consequence, a noticeable reduction of noncontact rate is usually observed. On the other hand, these characteristics of mobile devices make it more likely to reach a respondent at an inconvenient time and/or place, which leads to an increased refusal rate. Thus, the nonresponse rate is usually higher than in comparable landline surveys. Nevertheless, this difference is getting narrower according to an AAPOR (2010) report.

There are three components that contribute to nonresponse: noncontacts, refusals and undetermined eligibility. Given that sufficient call attempts are made (i.e. more than five), *noncontact* is about the same as in traditional landline surveys (AAPOR 2010). As mobile phone owners are reachable most of the day, the noncontact for mobile is decreasing; moreover, people who use their cell phones frequently have been observed to be more likely to participate in surveys (Brick et al. 2006). In contrast, for landlines noncontact is increasing as people tend to spend less time at home and an overload of unsolicited marketing and commercial communication is occurring. In addition Brick et al. (2006) found that frequent mobile phone users rarely answer their landline phones.

On the other hand, a disadvantage of mobile CATI is increased *refusals*, which are currently the main source of nonresponse (AAPOR 2010). The refusals can be due to different factors. First of all, mobile phones are considered tools for private and personal communication. However, this issue is becoming less important, since a more extent use of mobile devices for different purposes (e.g. business) is being observed. Second, the interviewed person can be charged for the incoming call (ESOMAR 2011) and, moreover, in some countries additional costs are applied for calls between different regions and across national boundaries. In this regard, unfortunately, reimbursing the respondents is often not an option due to technical limitations. However, the good news is that the increasing competition between operators in Europe is lowering the connection costs. Third, the variety of settings in which the respondent can be reached is also a factor pushing refusal rates, because they might not be willing to respond or might be busy (e.g. in a restaurant, during a meeting, while driving, etc.). Fourth, in general, and considering the previous three reasons as well, it is more difficult to convert a refusal in a mobile survey. However, this is not necessarily a drawback, since Groves and Peytcheva (2008) demonstrated that there is a risk of increasing the nonresponse bias while trying to reduce nonresponse.

Compared to landline phones, the *undetermined eligibility* factor is even more critical for mobile phones (AAPOR 2010). In fact, it can be very hard to determine the working status of a mobile device, and this for different reasons. First, it is not easy to determine the main purpose of the device, i.e. business/commercial or private. Second, the so-called 'churn' (i.e. the turnover of mobile numbers) is a more frequent phenomenon than for landlines, as it is easier to switch operators. Third, the irregular use of some mobile devices (e.g. for emergency calls only) is also making it harder to understand if the unit is eligible. Fourth, highly different automatic answering messages across wireless operators make it even harder to unambiguously classify the status of a phone number. The last two causes of unknown eligibility are becoming less relevant, due to a decrease of the sporadic use of mobile phones (e.g. for emergency purposes only) for the first cause and due to the consolidation of the industry, which is producing a more standardized message system across operators, for the second one.

A central issue within nonresponse studies is also *differential nonresponse*. Within mobile surveys it is characterized as an overestimated percentage of the mobile-only segment, as they have higher contact rates and lower refusal rates, if compared to those who own both a landline and a mobile phone (overlap). Moreover, the mobile-only respondents show a higher rate of completed interviews (AAPOR 2010). Differential nonresponse should be taken into account when weighting (see the next section).

Finally we briefly discuss measurement error, which is an additional component of survey error. In mobile phone interviews the measurement error is usually higher than in comparable landline surveys as accuracy is affected by the various contexts in which the survey is completed. For instance, the interviewee might be responding in a socially desirable way because they are in a public place, in particular if sensitive questions are asked. Moreover, due to noisy locations and bad volume settings, the respondent might have difficulties hearing and/or comprehending the questions asked by the interviewer, and the interviewer might also have difficulties hearing the answers. Furthermore, time constraints and concerns about the costs might press the respondent to rush through the interview and give less accurate answers. An important issue raised by Kennedy (2010) is that respondents might be distracted by being engaged in other activities while responding to a survey. Thus, to evaluate the quality of collected data, it is important to also ask questions about the context of the interview (AAPOR 2010; Lavrakas 2012). As Lavrakas (2012) showed, there is some indication that respondents who are away from home provide answers of poorer quality, even if, in general, mobility is not always associated with a higher measurement error.

Adjustment

Given the complex dual frame design and the issues associated with nonresponse and measurement error, it is necessary to weight data obtained by means of mobile CATI. Weighting is usually performed to account for different probabilities of selection, for differential propensities to respond and for coverage and/or sampling errors. A prerequisite for using the weighting approach for the problem of the dual frame overlap (already discussed in the previous "Mobile Phone Coverage" section) is having a good source of population estimates of phone status.

Different sources of phone use estimates exist both in Europe (Labour Force Survey, European Social Survey, Eurobarometer and Flash Eurobarometer) and in the US (Current Population Survey, National Health Interview Survey and Pew Research Centre). However, different sources use different question wordings to ask questions about phone use. Thus, for a given sample that we intend to weight we need to make sure that we replicate the same question wording as the source of estimates. Comparing question wordings in different sources (see **Table 4**, in the Appendix) we noted that these vary according to the definition of the device (i.e. working or non-working), of the device ownership (i.e. individual or household, personal or company) and, most importantly, according to the definition of use (i.e. possession or availability; see **Figure 4**). In some sources only the possession wording is used, in others only the availability one, while some use both. For instance, the Flash Eurobarometer (European Commission 2008) uses both the possession wording (e.g. 'Do you personally have a mobile/landline phone?') and the availability wording (e.g. 'Could I have reached you just now on your mobile/landline phone?'). Using Flash Eurobarometer data, Slavec and Vehovar (2011) showed that there are six groups of phone users (instead of the four listed in the "Mobile Phone Coverage" section). Two sub-groups are extracted from the overlap group. On one side, we have the mobile-mostly users, i.e. those that have both a landline and a mobile device but are in practice only reachable by a mobile phone. On the other hand, landline-mostly users are those that have both devices but are, in practice, only available through a landline phone.

Ownership

Availability

Landline-only

Has landline phone → Landline-mostly ← Is available by mobile phone

Overlap

Has cell phone → Mobile-mostly ← Is available by mobile phone

Mobile-only

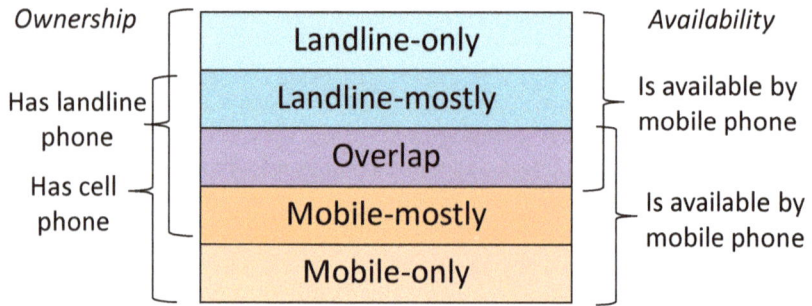

Figure 4: Additional groups of phone users (Source: Slavec & Vehovar 2011).

After selecting the population source, we need to select a weighting approach. In her work of 2011, Kennedy compared five different weighting approaches for dual frame samples:

1) *Simple 0.5 Compositing* (studied by Brick et al. 2006 and by Kennedy 2007), where the overlap is multiplied by 0.5, while the landline-only and mobile-only segments are not changed;

2) *Effective Sample Size Compositing* (Frankel et al. 2007), which integrates the overlap by weighting dual users proportionally to the effective sample size of the landline and mobile phone samples;

3) *Simple 0.5 Compositing with Modified Household Size* (Keeter, Christian & Dimock 2010), which is the same as the simple 0.5 compositing (1) but adjusted to household size;

4) *J. Best Raw Sample Size Compositing* (Best 2010), which is the most comprehensive approach as it creates a compositing factor from raw sample sizes by considering the probability of an adult to be selected in either the landline or the mobile sampling frame;

5) *Response Rate Compositing* (Brick et al. 2011), which adjusts for differential nonresponse in landline and mobile phone samples according to data on telephone possession and usage.

There is a bias/variance trade-off between the listed approaches: approaches 1) and 2) are better at reducing bias but they increase the design effect, whereas approaches 3) and 4) have a small design effect but their bias reduction is very small. A middle way is represented by the Response Rate Compositing (approach 5), which both reduces the bias and has a small design effect (Kennedy 2011).

Conclusions and further research

For every issue associated with using mobile CATI there is usually a very reasonable solution that is easy to apply.

Regarding legal and ethical issues, for example, the main suggestion would be to carefully check both the regulations and the legislations that characterize different countries in terms of respect for respondents (i.e. avoiding bothering them) and of their protection. Usually, the interview should start with questions to establish if it is safe and legal to involve the unit in the survey (e.g. asking if the respondent is driving or his/her age). Furthermore, to guarantee informed consent of the interviewee, the researchers should always clearly disclose detailed information about the main purposes of the survey and about the use of the collected data. There are a lot of documents with guidelines on ethical and legal issues to be followed by survey researchers, such as AAPOR (2010) and ESOMAR (2011) reports.

To sum up the coverage issues, we discussed three main topics. First, we introduced the differences between countries in terms of phone use according to the four groups in which the respondents can be classified: mobile only, landline only, overlap and no phone. Given the dissimilarities in the coverage of the four groups between countries and the socio-demographic differences that might appear while comparing the four groups, these issues should be studied in depth with further research and a solution should be appropriately chosen and applied in other phases of the survey (sampling and/or weighting). Second, for territorial coverage the main issues could be faced by simply asking questions about residential information. Similarly, this method can also be applied to the third issue, the within-household coverage, for which we should ask information about the primary user and the purpose of use of the device.

Like landline CATI, mobile CATI requires either telephone registers or random digit dialing. In many cases, multiple frame sampling is recommended, which requires dealing with the overlap of mobile and landline phone users. A weighting approach is recommended, at least for populations for which telephone status estimates are available, whereas the screening approach is the only option when no accurate estimates of telephone status exist.

It appears that higher nonresponse is an issue with mobile phone surveys; however, the difference between landline and mobile nonresponse is actually decreasing, and it may disappear in few years. This decrease is mainly caused by the decreasing noncontact rate, since most of the respondents are reachable through their devices almost all the time. However, the refusals are higher due to the diverse and distracting settings in which a respondent can be contacted. For the same reason measurement error is also gradually increasing. Coming back to nonresponse, there are more units for which it is not easy to determine eligibility; however, the extent of this problem is diminishing with the evolution of mobile phone industry and usage. Lastly it is also important to take into consideration the differential nonresponse between different groups according to their phone status by appropriately weighting data.

The discussed coverage, sampling, nonresponse and measurement issues should be faced with an appropriate weighting approach. Taking into account the variance/bias trade-off, the best approach is the Response Rate Compositing.

This, and other approaches as well, requires accurate population estimates. In case they are not available, researchers should better use the screening approach when combining landline and mobile surveys.

To conclude, further research about how to integrate mobile phones in survey research is highly needed, along with a more thorough discussion of the various issues that we summarized in this chapter. As a prerequisite, more surveys should include questions about mobile phone use, respondents' reachability, their preferences and device availability. This will enable researchers to better design mobile phone surveys and to properly integrate them with other research modes, considering the specificities and regulations that characterize different countries as well.

Appendix

Country	2004	2006	2007/8	2009	2011	2013	Nine-year changes
AT	22.5	40.2	41.6	48.0	49.3	60.6	+38.1
BE	20.7	29.0	30.3	33.8	30.7	32.4	+11.7
BG	7.7	17.6	19.1	31.6	42.1	54.3	+46.6
CY	5.7	14.4	14.2	16.1	15.5	24.8	+19.1
CZ	34.9	53.0	62.6	73.5	80.1	84.3	+49.5
DE	5.2	8.7	10.4	9.8	8.9	10.9	+5.6
DK	10.2	17.4	21.2	31.2	37.1	43.8	+33.6
EE	36.4	46.5	40.3	44.8	49.0	57.1	+20.6
ES	15.2	22.7	24.4	29.3	26.9	31.7	+16.5
FI	33.5	53.8	62.3	71.7	78.3	85.8	+52.3
FR	12.9	17.9	14.2	10.3	11.9	10.7	−2.1
GB	9.1	12.3	12.6	19.2	14.0	15.6	+6.5
GR	9.7	17.1	17.8	20.2	15.7	16.8	+7.0
HU	27.6	42.6	48.3	46.0	47.4	49.7	+22.1
IE	12.1	23.4	19.4	27.0	31.1	38.7	+26.5
IT	23.9	39.6	37.8	29.8	32.3	31.8	+8.0
LT	46.1	49.2	53.1	54.7	61.3	68.3	+22.2
LU	5.5	6.3	4.0	9.2	8.6	13.3	+7.8
LV	32.2	44.6	45.5	49.9	50.0	67.1	+34.9
MT	3.2	3.9	3.9	2.1	2.5	4.0	+0.9
NL	2.4	6.7	8.2	10.3	9.8	12.1	+9.6
PL	15.5	24.7	31.6	42.8	48.3	62.1	+46.6
PT	37.3	34.9	46.1	40.5	34.8	47.1	+9.8
RO	15.0	34.4	35.2	42.0	50.2	57.9	+42.9
SE	0.3	2.4	2.3	0.6	2.0	2.3	+2.0
SI	12.0	12.4	14.6	17.0	16.7	26.9	+15.0
SK	41.4	43.0	49.0	57.6	61.1	77.1	+35.7

Table 2: Mobile-only category: percentages (from 2004 to 2013) and nine-year changes (in percentage points) according to Eurobarometer data (European Commission 2012a, 2012b, 2012c, 2013a, 2013b, 2013c).

	Mobile only	Overlap	Landline only	No phone	Total
AT	60.6	33.9	4.8	0.6	100
BE	32.4	59.4	7.6	0.7	100
BG	54.3	32.9	7.3	5.6	100
CY	24.8	73.0	2.2	0.0	100
CZ	84.3	12.1	0.8	2.8	100
DE	10.9	80.4	8.4	0.4	100
DK	43.8	53.1	2.5	0.6	100
EE	57.1	39.0	2.4	1.5	100
ES	31.7	55.4	9.5	3.5	100
FI	85.8	12.2	1.2	0.8	100
FR	10.7	79.2	9.9	0.2	100
GB	15.6	76.0	7.6	0.8	100
GR	16.8	73.8	8.9	0.6	100
HR	17.2	68.0	13.4	1.4	100
HU	49.7	38.5	7.6	4.2	100
IE	38.7	56.3	2.4	2.6	100
IT	31.8	61.9	4.9	1.3	100
LT	68.3	24.7	3.8	3.2	100
LU	13.3	84.1	2.5	0.0	100
LV	67.1	28.8	1.8	2.2	100
MT	4.0	89.1	6.9	0.0	100
NL	12.1	81.9	5.9	0.2	100
PL	62.1	25.6	7.0	5.3	100
PT	47.1	32.0	14.3	6.7	100
RO	57.9	26.9	7.4	7.8	100
SE	2.3	93.5	3.9	0.3	100
SI	26.9	66.2	6.3	0.6	100
SK	77.1	13.4	2.0	7.6	100

Table 3: Structure of the four groups in 2013.

Survey	Landline phone possesion wording	Mobile phone possesion wording
Eurobarometer	Do you own a fixed telephone in your household?	Do you own a personal mobile telephone?
Flash EB	[Mobile subsample] – D11b. Do you have a fixed telephone at home?	[Landline subsample] – D11a. Do you personally have a mobile phone?
Labour Force Survey	F71. Does your household have a fixed phone?	F72. Do you have your own mobile phone (including company mobile phone)?
European Social Survey	DOD1. Is there a fixed-line telephone in (your part of) this accommodation? (Note: "your part of" refers to separate 'households' living in the same building, not rooms within a household)	DOD2. Do you personally have a mobile telephone?
Current Population Survey (Tucker et al. 2007)	Q1. […] How many different landline telephone numbers does your household have? Q1a. Excluding any numbers used only for faxes and computers, how many of these (Q1) landline phones are used for incoming calls?	Q2. Do you or any other members of your household have a working cellular phone number?
National Health Interview Survey (Brick et al. 2011)	N1. Is there at least one telephone inside your home that is currently working and is not a cellular phone?	N2. Does anyone in your family have a working cellular telephone?
California Health Interview Survey 2007 (Brick et. al 2011)	[Mobile subsample] – CC1. Is this cell phone your only phone or do you also have a regular telephone at home?	[Landline subsample] – CL1. Do you have a working cell phone?
California Health Interview Survey 2005 (Brick et. al. 2007)	[Mobile subsample] – Is this cell phone your only phone or do you also have a regular telephone at home?	/
Pew 2008/09 (Brick et al. 2011)	[Mobile subsample] – PC1. Now thinking about your telephone use … Is there at least one telephone INSIDE your home that is currently working and is not a cell phone?	[Landline subsample] – PL1. Now thinking about your telephone use … Do you have a working cell phone?
Pew 2006 and (Keeter et. al. 2007)	[Mobile subsample] – Is the cell phone your only phone or do you also have a regular telephone at home?	[Landline subsample] – Do you happen to have a cell phone or not?

Table 4: Phone possession question wording in different surveys (Source: Slavec and Vehovar 2011).

Acknowledgement

We would like to acknowledge WebDataNet (COST Action IS1004, http:// webdatanet.cbs.dk/), the University of Bergamo (60% University funds) and and University of Ljubljana.

References

AAPOR Cell Phone Task Force. (2010). *New Considerations for Survey Researchers When Planning and Conduction RDD Telephone Surveys in the U.S. With Respondents Reached via Cell Phone Numbers.*

Arthur, A. (2007). The birth of a cellular nation. New York: Mediamark Research.

Best, J. (2010). *First-Stage Weights for Overlapping Dual Frame Telephone Survey.* Paper presented at the Annual Conference of the American Association for Public Opinion Research, Chicago, IL, USA.

Blumberg S. J., & **Luke, J. V.** (2009). *Wireless substitution: Early release of estimates from the National Health Interview Survey, July–December 2008.* National Center for Health Statistics. Retrieved 29 July 2010 from http:// www.cdc.gov/nchs/nhis.htm

Blumberg, S. J., & **Luke, J. V.** (2013). *Wireless Substitution: Early Release of Estimates From the National Health Interview Survey, January–June 2013.* Retrieved July 18, 2014, from http://www.cdc.gov/nchs/data/nhis/early release/wireless201312.pdf

Brick, J. M. (2009). *Dual Frame Theory Applied to Landline and Cell Phone Surveys.* American Statistical Association Survey Research Methods Section Webinar.

Brick, J. M., Dipko, S., Presser, S., Tucker, C., & **Yangyang, Y.** (2005). *Estimation Issues in Dual Frame Sample of Cell and Landline Numbers.* ASA Section on Survey Research Methods. http://www.amstat.org/sections/srms/ proceedings/y2005/files/jsm2005-000236.pdf

Brick, J. M., Dipko, S., Presser, S., Tucker, C., & **Yangyang, Y.** (2006). Nonresponse bias in a Dual Frame Sample of Cell and Landline Numbers. *Public Opinion Quarterly, 70*(5). Retrieved October 26, 2009, from http:// poq.oxfordjournals.org/cgi/content/ abstract/70/5/780. DOI: http://dx.doi. org/10.1093/poq/nfl031.

Brick, J. M., Sherman W. E., & **Sunghee, L.** (2007). Sampling telephone numbers and dults, interview length, and weighting in the California health interview survey cell phone pilot study. *Public Opinion Quarterly* 71(51):793-813.

Brick, J.M., Cervantes, F.I., Lee, S., & **Norman, G.** (2011). Nonsampling Errors in Dual Frame Telephone Surveys. *Survey methodology, 37*(1), 1–12.

Busse, B., & Fuchs, M. (2012). The components of landline telephone survey coverage bias. The relative importance of non-phone and mobile-only populations. *Quality and Quantity, 46*(4), 1209–1225. DOI: http://dx.doi.org/10.1007/s11135-011-9431-3

CAN-SPAM Act. (2003). Retrieved July 14, 2014, from http://www.gpo.gov/fdsys/pkg/PLAW-108publ187/html/PLAW-108publ187.htm

ESOMAR. (1999). Interviewing children and young people. Retrieved July 16, 2014, from http://www.esomar.org/uploads/public/knowledge-and-standards/codes-and-guidelines/ESOMAR_Codes-and-Guidelines_Interviewing-Children-and-Young-People.pdf

ESOMAR. (2011). ICC/ESOMAR International Code on market and Social Research: Esomar guideline for conducting survey research via mobile phone. Retrieved July 15, 2014, from http://www.esomar.org/uploads/public/knowledge-and-standards/codes-and-guidelines/ESOMAR_Guideline-for-conducting-Research-via-Mobile-Phone.pdf

ESOMAR. (2013). Summary of regulations covering unsolicited contacts. Retrieved July 14, 2014, from http://www.esomar.org/uploads/professional_standards/guidelines/ESOMAR-Codes&Guidelines-Legislative-issues-unsolicited-contacts.pdf

European Commission. (2008). *Flash Eurobarometer 251. Public attitudes and perceptions in the Euro area.* Brussels: Gallup Europe [Producer]. Cologne: GESIS [Publisher]. ZA4743, data set version 2.0.0. Description. Retrieved 29 July 2010 from http://info1.gesis.org/dbksearch13/ sdesc2.asp?no=4743&db=e&doi=10.4232/1.10007

European Commission. (2012a). *Eurobarometer 68.2, December 2007-January 2008.* TNS OPINION & SOCIAL, Brussels [Producer]; GESIS Data Archive: ZA4742, dataset version 4.0.1

European Commission. (2012b). *Eurobarometer 66.3, November-December 2006.* TNS OPINION & SOCIAL, Brussels [Producer]; GESIS Data Archive: ZA4528, dataset version 2.0.1

European Commission. (2012c). *Eurobarometer 62.2, November-December 2004.* TNS OPINION & SOCIAL, Brussels [Producer]; GESIS Data Archive: ZA4231, dataset version 1.1.0

European Commission. (2013a). *Eurobarometer 69.1, May-June 2013.* TNS OPINION & SOCIAL, Brussels [Producer]; GESIS Data Archive: ZA5852, dataset version 2.0.0

European Commission. (2013b). *Eurobarometer 75.1, February-March 2011.* TNS OPINION & SOCIAL, Brussels [Producer]; GESIS Data Archive: ZA5479, dataset version 6.0.0

European Commission. (2013c). *Eurobarometer 72.5, November-December 2009.* TNS OPINION & SOCIAL, Brussels [Producer]; GESIS Data Archive: ZA4999, dataset version 5.1.0

Frankel, M.R., Battaglia, M.P., Link, M., & Mokdad, A. H. (2007). Integrating Cell Phone Numbers into Random Digit Dial (RDD) Landline Surveys. *ASA Proceedings of the Social Statistics Section,* 3793–3800.

Fuchs, M. (2002). Kann man Umfragen per Handy durchführen? Ausschöpfung, Interview-Dauer und Item-Nonresponse im Vergleich mit einer Festnetz-Stichprobe [Is it feasible to conduct surveys with mobile phone? Participation, duration of interview and item non-response in comparison to a landline sample]. *Planung und Analyse, 29*(2), 57–63.

Fuchs, M., & Busse, B. (2009). The coverage bias of mobile web surveys across european countries. *International Journal of Internet Science, 4,* 21–33.

Groves, R. M., Fowler, F. J., Couper, M. P., Lepkowski, J. M., Singer, E., Tourangeau, R. (2004). *Survey methodology.* Hoboken, NJ: Wiley.

Groves, R. M., & Peytcheva, E. (2008). The Impact of Nonresponse Rates on Nonresponse Bias - A Meta-Analysis. *Public Opinion Quarterly, 72*(2), 167–189. DOI: http://dx.doi.org/10.1093/poq/nfn011

Grünwald, C. A. (2013, September). *Legal and ethical implications of social media and online research.* Paper presented at the 6th WEBDATANET meeting, Reykjavik, Iceland.

Jones, C. (2011). *Ethical issues in online research.* British Educational Research Association on-line resource. Retrieved July 14, 2014, from http://www.bera.ac.uk/wp-content/uploads/2014/03/Ethical-issues-in-online-research.pdf

Keeter, S., Kennedy, C., Clark, A., Tompson, T., & Mokrzycki, M. (2007). What's missing from National RDD Surveys? The impact of growin Cell-only Population. *Public Opinion Quarterly* 71(5): 772-792.

Keeter, S., Christian, L., & Dimock, M. (2010). The Growing Gap between Landline and Dual Frame Election Polls: Republican Vote Share Bigger in Landline-Only Surveys. Retrieved July 18, 2014, from http://www.pewresearch.org/2010/11/22/the-growing-gap-between-landline-and-dual-frame-election-polls

Kennedy, C. (2007). Evaluating the Effects of Screening for Telephone Service in Dual Frame RDD Surveys. *Public Opinion Quarterly, 71*(5). Retrieved October 26, 2009, from http://poq.oxfordjournals.org/cgi/content/abstract/71/5/750. DOI: http://dx.doi.org/10.1093/poq/nfm050

Kennedy, C. (2010). *Nonresponse and Measurement Error in Mobile Phone Survey* (Doctoral dissertation, University of Michigan, Ann Arbor).

Kennedy, C. (2011). *An evaluation of popular weighting approaches in dual frame RDD surveys.* Paper presented at the 66th conference of the American Association for Public Opinion Research, Phoenix, AZ, USA.

Lavrakas, P.J. (2012). *Measures of Data Quality Across the RDD Frames.* SRC Workshop, Melbourne, Australia.

Nicolai, S. (2009). Representativity of mobile data collection based on the example of Germany. In N. Döring, A. Ließ, & E. Maxl (Eds.), *Mobile market research* (pp. 205–216). Köln: Herbert von Halem.

Poggio, T., & Callegaro, M. (2012). Italy. In S. Häder, M. Häder, & M. Kühne (Eds.), *Telephone Surveys in Europe.* Springer.

Slavec, A., & Vehovar, V. (2011). *Optimization of dual frame telephone survey designs.* Paper presented at the 4th Conference of the European Survey Research Association (ESRA), Lausanne, Switzerland.

Tucker, C., Brick, M. J., & Meekins, B. (2007). Household telephone service and usage patterns in the United States in 2004: Implications for telephone samples. *Public Opinion Quarterly* 71(1):3-22.

Vehovar , V., & Slavec, A. (2012). Preference for Mobile Interview Surveys? Interplay of Costs, Errors and Biases. In S. Häder, M. Häder, & M. Kühne (Eds.), *Telephone Surveys in Europe.* Springer.

CHAPTER 5

Comparison of Response Times between Desktop and Smartphone Users

Ioannis Andreadis

Aristotle University of Thessaloniki, Greece,
john@auth.gr

Abstract

This chapter offers a precise and thoroughly tested estimate of the impact of using a smartphone on item response times. The comparison is made between desktop and smartphone users when they use a voting advice application that was specifically designed to be used on smartphones. The analysis shows that i) after taking into account item and user characteristics that are known to affect response times and ii) using the most suitable statistical models, using a smartphone instead of a desktop is expected to increase by 17% the geometric mean of item response times.

Keywords

web surveys, item response times, smartphones, multilevel models, endogeneity, generalized structural equation models

Introduction

The aim of this chapter is to test if web survey item response times differ between desktop and smartphone users. Item response times and total response times of web surveys have attracted the attention of many researchers recently, because longer web surveys suffer from larger break-off rates and greater probability of

How to cite this book chapter:
Andreadis, I. 2015. Comparison of Response Times between Desktop and Smartphone Users. In:Toninelli, D, Pinter, R & de Pedraza, P (eds.) *Mobile Research Methods: Opportunities and Challenges of Mobile Research Methodologies*, Pp. 63–79. London: Ubiquity Press. DOI: http://dx.doi.org/10.5334/bar.e. License: CC-BY 4.0.

lower quality responses near the end of the questionnaire due to respondents' fatigue. In addition, during the last few years, web survey researchers have observed that the number of people who use mobile devices to participate in web surveys is increasing rapidly. Therefore, many recent publications study the implications of responding to web surveys while using mobile devices.

Mavletova (2013), analyzing an experiment with two survey modes conducted using a volunteer online access panel in Russia, reports that the mean time of questionnaire completion for mobile surveys was three times longer than the mean time for computer web surveys, and she presents three possible reasons for this large difference: i) slower Internet connection, ii) limited functionality of the cell phone (smaller screen size and lack of mouse and keyboard) and iii) greater probability of facing distractions for respondents completing the survey outside of their home. On the other hand, Toepoel and Lugtig (2014), offering a mobile-friendly option to respondents to an online probability-based panel organized by a research consultancy agency in the Netherlands, find that the total response times are almost the same across devices and that the mean values differ only by five seconds (245s on desktop, 250s on mobile). These contradictory findings cannot be attributed to country-specific characteristics only (e.g. differences of mobile Internet speed between the Netherlands and Russia), because de Bruijne and Wijnant (2013), after running an experiment with CentERpanel participants (also in the Netherlands and also with a mobile-friendly environment), compare the completion time between groups and find that there is a significant difference, i.e. the respondents required more time to finish the survey on a mobile device than on a computer, but they also find mixed results when they compare item response times between devices.

Couper and Peterson (2015) use both server- and client-level times in order to disentangle between-page (transmission) times from within-page (response) times, and they report that mobile respondents took significantly longer to complete the survey than PC respondents, and that most of this difference is due to within-page times. In compliance with their finding I argue that transmission times are less important than response times for two reasons: i) issues related to the speed of mobile Internet will eventually be eliminated as mobile Internet providers improve their services and ii) new technologies enable web survey designers to download the next pages of the questionnaire to the users' browser before these pages are requested, thereby eliminating any transmission delays. Thus, the focus of this chapter is on the time that the respondent really spends interacting with the questionnaire, reading and answering questions, and excludes transmission times.

Some of the respondents' characteristics that are known to affect response times, such as age and education level (Couper & Kreuter 2013; Yan & Tourangeau 2008), have been reported to also affect mobile web access (de Bruijne & Wijnant 2013; Fuchs & Busse 2009; Gummer & Roßmann 2014). Since mobile web access is not randomly distributed across the population, for the data analysis presented in this chapter, I employ advanced models where completing the survey using a mobile device is treated as an endogenous variable while taking into account, in addition to the aforementioned respondent characteristics, some item characteristics that are known to have an impact on the response time, such as the length of the question text (see Andreadis 2012 and Andreadis 2014a).

Data

The findings presented in this chapter are based on the analysis of the paradata collected in May 2014 by the Greek Voting Advice Application (VAA) HelpMeVote – VoteMatch Greece (Andreadis 2013), which is the Greek part of the multi-national European project VoteMatch (votematch.eu) used for the elections for the European Parliament. Voting advice applications are special types of opt-in web surveys that help users find their proximities with political parties. In the period before an election, these applications can become very popular, and they attract thousands or even millions of users. HelpMeVote is a web application based on jQuery Mobile. As a result, HelpMeVote is compatible with all major mobile platforms and all major desktop browsers. It is able to run both on PCs and on mobile devices; it automatically scales to any screen size and it supports both touch and mouse events. The user interface follows the most common features of designing for mobile devices, e.g. large font size and large buttons. Finally, the question texts are short and the number of response options is limited and displayed vertically to eliminate the need for horizontal scrolling.

HelpMeVote for the European Elections 2014 includes 31 questions, and each question is displayed on a separate page, but it is built as an AJAX application and all pages are downloaded from the beginning to the users' browser. This means that there is no lag time between answering one question and viewing the next one. Consequently, the time between clicks can be counted accurately. The response times are recorded in hidden input fields. Communication with the server is done in the end, when all questions have been answered and the user clicks the 'Submit' button. When the respondent submits the web page, the content of the hidden fields (i.e. response timestamps) are transmitted to the server and are stored in a database along with the User-Agent header of the user's browser. Thus, it is possible to compare between desktop and mobile device users using accurately measured response times and a very large dataset (consisting of tens of thousands of cases).

According to Hypertext Transfer Protocol (HTTP) (see Fielding, Berners-Lee & Frystyk 1996) the User-Agent header field contains information about the user agent originating a HTTP request. For the purposes of this chapter, I have used PHP[21] to retrieve the HTTP_USER_AGENT element of the $_SERVER array,

---

[21] PHP is an open source scripting language especially suited for web development that can be embedded into HTML: http://php.net/.

and I have linked this information with each respondent in the database. Then, using the PHP function get_browser() I have determined the capabilities of the user's browser.[22] By using the aforementioned PHP function I can get the type of the device that the user has used to access the web server. At the time of writing this chapter using the Browser Capabilities Project, the device type field can get one of the following values: Mobile Phone, Mobile Device, Tablet, Desktop, TV Device, Console, FonePad, Ebook Reader, Car Entertainment System or Unknown.

Dealing with extremely short response times

In a previous paper, I provide a formula that can be used to flag responses which were given so quickly that the response is probably not valid (Andreadis 2014a). The method uses the decomposition of the survey response process into four major tasks given by Tourangeau, Rips and Rasinski (2000): 1) comprehension of the question, 2) retrieval of relevant information, 3) use of that information to render the judgment and 4) selection and reporting of an answer. For the estimation of the minimum time needed for Task 1 I used the table provided by Carver (1992) connecting reading speed rates and three types of reading: rauding, skimming and scanning. Bassili and Fletcher (1991), using an active timer, have found that on average, simple attitude questions take between 1.4 and 2 seconds to answer, and more complex attitude questions take between 2 and 2.6 seconds. In their experiment, time counting starts when the interviewer presses the spacebar after reading the last word of the question. Time counting stops with a voice-key (the first noise that comes from the respondent's side triggers the computer to read the clock). For VAAs and web surveys time counting stops when the user clicks on one of the available buttons that correspond to answer options. This additional step requires some extra time. Thus, the minimum time reported by Bassili and Fletcher (1991) for simple attitude questions (1.4 seconds) can be used as the minimum time for Task 4 (selecting and reporting the answer).

If all questions included in a VAA have similar complexity, then the most significant factor that affects the time spent on Task 1 is the length of the question. These two quantities (length and time) are proportional, and their ratio defines the reading speed. VAA users need time to read the sentence using a reading speed suitable for the comprehension of the ideas in the sentence. Andreadis (2014a) calculates a threshold that can be used to flag items that

---

[22] The function looks up the browser's information in a large file that includes a list of all known browsers and bots, along with their default capabilities and limitations. The file is provided by the Browser Capabilities Project, also known as 'browscap' or 'BCP'. The file is provided in several formats, but the most commonly used is named browscap.ini and is available at: http://browscap.org/

were responded to in an extremely short time using the following formula: threshold = 1.4+[number of characters in the item]/39.375.

Using the same formula I have flagged the answers of HelpMeVote 2014 that have been given in less than the time given by the threshold as extremely short response times. Then I have counted the number of extremely short response times for each user. If more than one third of the response times of a user were extremely short, I removed the corresponding case from the dataset. The reason for the decision to eliminate the complete records of these users is that these users were found to give extremely fast responses so many times that there is strong evidence that they are not using the VAA in a normal way, but they are probably just testing or playing with the application. Thus, the rest of their answers, although they have not been flagged as extremely fast, are probably invalid, and it is better to remove them.

Dealing with extremely long response times

By observing the cases with extremely short response times we can find users who display a more or less stable speeding behavior while responding to a large number of items. The picture for extremely long response times is very different. It is very rare to observe a user spending extremely long times to answer the majority of questions. In most cases a user has spent extremely long times on a very limited number of items. This difference between extremely long and extremely short times has a very good explanation: extremely short times are the result of a decision made by users who decide to respond without paying too much attention (or even any at all) to the questions; these users usually maintain the same attitude throughout the questionnaire. On the other hand, extremely long times are the result of an interruption that usually occurs after an external distraction (e.g. an incoming email, a phone call, someone knocking at the door, etc). Thus, the occurrence of extremely long response times is associated neither with a user nor with an item. Of course, longer items require longer response times, but a typical questionnaire would not include an item which is so long that it could require an extremely long time to read. Thus, the occurrence of extremely long response times is random and it can be identified both by looking for extremely long times per item and by looking for extremely long times per user. Taking into account that a typical VAA includes about 30 items and is used by thousands or even millions of users, it is easier to look for extremely long times within each user.

A good way to look for extreme response times within a user is to use the methods of exploratory data analysis, and more specifically the statistics used for boxplots (Hoaglin, Mosteller & Tukey 1983; McGill, Tukey & Larsen 1978; Tukey 1977). Boxplot statistics can identify outliers, i.e. values between the inner and the outer fences of the boxplot, and extreme values, i.e. values outside the outer fences. As outer fences, I use the values: $Q_1 - 3 \times IQR$ and

Q_3 + 3×IQR, where IQR is the interquartile range and Q1 and Q3 are the first and the third quartiles, respectively. The problem of applying this method on the response times themselves is that it would flag as extreme too many values that are not extreme.

The distribution of response times is a semi-bounded function with zero as its lower bound. Usually it is highly skewed to the right. The logarithmic function is a good way of transforming a highly skewed distribution into one that is closer to normal distribution. Thus, in order to flag the real extremely large response times, I have applied the logarithmic function to the response times and then I have applied the aforementioned exploratory data analysis method to identify extreme values on the logs of the response times.

After flagging the extremely long response times, there is one last decision to be made: How should they be treated? I argue that they should be recoded as missing values. The logic behind this argument is very simple. We cannot leave them intact, because the recorded time is not the actual time spent on the question but the sum of the time spent on answering the question, plus an unknown amount of time due to some external distraction. We should not remove the whole record, because we do not have a user giving invalid answers (as was the case with extremely short response times). Thus, the best way of dealing with these values is to consider them as missing, because the external distraction that interrupted the user has prevented us from recording the actual time spent on the item. By recoding the extremely long response times as missing, we do not allow them to distort the average response times estimated by the sample. At the same time we do not have to disregard the whole row, because we can use these records with statistical methods that do not require list-wise deletion of cases with missing values or we can impute the missing values using the response times of the same user on the rest of the items.

Other data preparations

HelpMeVote users answer 31 questions in order to get their proximity with the Greek political parties. Before being given the output, users are asked to fill in a form with their personal information (mostly demographics, i.e. Sex, Age Group, Education Level, but also information related to their voting behavior, i.e. Vote Choice, Political Interest). Although it is not mandatory (users can click 'continue' and move on to the output without answering) the vast majority responds to most of these questions,[23] probably because they are in a responsive mood or because they consider this form as part of the VAA procedure[24].

---

[23] Vote Choice is the only item in this form that displays a large number of non-useful answers because many users either give no answer or indicate that they have not decided yet.

[24] HelpMeVote offers an 'info' page where users are informed that their responses are stored in a database anonymously to be used for academic research.

For the analysis presented in this chapter, I have kept only the cases where the demographic variables have valid values. There are three reasons which support a decision to remove the cases with missing values on demographic variables: i) the percentage of missing values is very small, ii) these variables will be used as predictors for the models in the following sections and iii) imputing the missing value of demographic variables from the answers to the rest of the questions is difficult.

More than 80,000 HelpMeVote/VoteMatch 2014 questionnaires have been completed by Greek citizens during the period before the elections for the European Parliament. In order to work with a sample that can be handled by the computational resources of a strong workstation, I had to randomly select a subsample corresponding to 10% of the total sample. In order to ensure that the findings presented in this chapter are the same as the findings that I would present if I had used the total sample I have done the following tests: i) I have checked and I have verified that the distributions of the main variables in the subsample are not different from the corresponding distributions in the total sample and ii) I have replicated the presented analysis with other 10% subsamples and I have got very similar findings. The used sample is available from OpenICPSR (Andreadis 2014b).

Finally, the distribution of the used devices is as follows: 80.7% desktops, 13.5% smartphones and 5.7% other mobile devices (mostly tablets). The focus of this chapter is on the comparison between smartphone and desktop users. Therefore, the users of other mobile devices have been excluded from the analysis.

Variables

In the following models the logarithm of the response times is used as the dependent variable (i.e. the outcome). As the main task of this chapter is to compare the response times between smartphone users and desktop users, the binary variable 'mobile' is included in the model as the main treatment under study.

As control variables from the item characteristics, I use the length of the statement and a dummy variable that takes the value of 1 when the statement is about an EU issue and 0 when the statement is about a national issue. The inclusion of the latter variable is justified by the fact that Greek voters are presumed to be less informed about EU policy issues than they are about national issues, and they are expected to need more time to express their opinion about EU issues.

From users' characteristics I use as control dummy variables taking the value of 1 for male respondents, for people aged over 49 years old (over49), for users who are interested in politics (polint) and for citizens who had already made their vote choice when they used the VAA (decided). According to the literature my hypotheses about these predictors are as follows: older people (> 49) are expected to spend more time than younger people. Citizens interested in politics and voters who have already decided their vote choice should be more familiar with the major issues of the electoral competition, so they are expected to have clear, pre-formulated opinions about the statements, and they are expected to need less time than people not interested in politics and people who had not decided about their vote choice when they used HelpMeVote. Finally some studies have found that female respondents spend more time on web surveys, thus I expect a similar finding from the present analysis. As a final user characteristic, I use the education level as a categorical variable, and I compare all other education categories with the category of primary education (used as the reference category). The expectation here is that as we switch to higher education levels, the response time should decrease.

Unfortunately, the treatment variable of the model (mobile) is endogenous, and it depends on variables that also affect the outcome (e.g. age). In order to correctly estimate the treatment effect, I employ advanced statistical methods (described in the following section). In order to model the endogeneity of the treatment I use as its predictor the age dummy variable 'over49', but I do not use the education level because I have not found the education level to have an impact on the treatment variable. I also use a variable named 'scorex' which indicates the position of the user on the political left/right axis, because I have found that it is a good predictor of using a smartphone (as users move from the left to the right of the axis, they tend to use smartphones more), while it does not have an impact on response times.

Methods

Smartphone web access is not randomly distributed across the population. Thus in order to study the impact of using a smartphone on item response times, I had to employ a constrained endogenous-switching model (also known as endogenous treatment-effects model), i.e. a model where the treatment (completing the survey using a smartphone) is considered as an endogenous variable (Greene 2012; Heckman 1978; Maddala 1983; Wooldridge 2010). In these models, instead of having a single linear equation for the prediction of the outcome, I have two equations. The first is the linear equation for the outcome. The treatment is a binary variable that is considered to take the values 0 or 1 when a latent variable is smaller or larger than 0, respectively. This latent variable is also given by a linear equation. The error terms of these two linear equations follow a joint bivariate normal distribution, and they are allowed to be correlated. The coefficient for this correlation can be estimated by the endogenous treatment-effects model. If the estimated correlation between the treatment errors and the outcome errors is significant (i.e. if we reject the null hypothesis of no correlation) then the impact of the treatment on the outcome cannot be estimated correctly by a simple model and we have to use the estimates provided by the advanced model. On the other hand, if the advanced model indicates that the correlation coefficient is not statistically significant, we can use the estimates of the simple, single equation model.

At the same time I had to take into account other factors that are known to have an impact on item response time. These factors are characteristics of the respondent, e.g. gender, age, education, interest in the theme of the survey, knowledge about the survey topics; and characteristics of the items, such as the length or the difficulty of the item. There are two levels in the model: the respondent level and the item level. The usual approach is to consider the items as the lower level and the respondents as the higher level, i.e. to consider a hierarchical linear model where the items are nested within the respondents (van der Linden 2008), but there are example of reversed roles, i.e. where the hierarchical model is built on the basis that respondents are nested within items (Swanson et al. 2001). The item response times within the same user may be correlated (intraclass correlation) due to individual characteristics (e.g. education) that affect reading speed. As a result, the assumption of independence of the observations is violated. Using a non-hierarchical model would underestimate the standard errors of regression coefficients – especially for the coefficients of the user level predictors – resulting in non statistically significant coefficients to appear as significant (Gelman & Hill 2006; Hox 2002). Another advantage of using a multilevel model is that the residual variance is partitioned into a between-user and a within-user component. Consequently, by using a multilevel model, it is possible to study the effects of both user level and item level characteristics, get better estimates of the standard errors of the regression coefficients and compare the between-user with the within-user variance.

For the data analysis of this chapter I needed an endogenous treatment-effects multilevel regression model. To my knowledge, there are not any out-of-the-box regression procedures that can be used for the estimation of this complicated model in any of the statistical (either commercial or open source) software packages. According to Skrondal and Rabe-Hesketh (2004) a way to deal with this problem is to use generalized Structural Equation Modeling (SEM). Structural models are able to show causal dependencies between endogenous and exogenous variables. This means that structural equation models can be used as alternatives to the systems of regression equations (such as the endogenous treatment-effects model) used by Heckman (1978) and other econometricians. With generalized structural equation modeling we can generalize Heckman models (both selection and endogenous treatment models) to include multilevel effects. The corresponding structural equation model includes two equations, one linear regression (to model the outcome) and a censored regression (for the treatment selection model). By adding a common latent variable in both equations we can model the correlation between them. By constraining the latent variable to have variance and coefficient in the selection equation both equal to 1 and the variance from the censored regression equal to the variance of the linear regression we can have an identified model.

The multilevel structure can be modeled in SEM by including a random intercept at the user level. This is done by adding a latent variable that is constant within users and varies across users and a path from this latent variable to the outcome variable. For details on estimating multilevel linear models as structural equation models the interested reader can consult the related literature by Bauer (2003) and Curran (2003). For the technical details see also the book by Skrondal and Rabe-Hesketh (2004).

In the following section I present a generalized SEM. This is a very complicated model that takes into account both the endogeneity and the multilevel structure of the dataset, i.e. it is a generalized structural equation model that represents an endogenous treatment-effects multi-level regression. This model requires a tremendous amount of computer resources (both CPU power and memory), and I had to randomly select a subset of the data to run this complicated analysis. As mentioned before, I have verified the findings presented in the next section by running the analysis again on additional random subsamples.

Findings

As I have already explained in the previous section, since the treatment is endogenous, we need a generalized structural equation model that represents an endogenous treatment-effects multi-level regression. This model is presented in **Figure 1**. The main question in these models is whether the correlation between the error terms of the equations is significant. This question is important because if the correlation is not significant, we can forget about the endogeneity of the treatment variable and we can use a simpler model, such as a multilevel linear regression. As **Table 1** indicates, the value of the correlation coefficient ρ is estimated at 0.011 and the corresponding test shows that it is not significantly different from 0 (the p-value of the test is 0.937). This means that we do not need the censored regression and we can use the estimates of a simpler model.

Figure 2 and **Table 2** show the generalized structural equation model that is equivalent to a multilevel regression. **Figure 2** includes the estimated coefficients and the estimated values for the error terms. **Table 2** shows the exponential values of the coefficients. Since I have used the logarithm of the response times as the outcome of the model, the interpretation of the estimated regression coefficients is the following: if the estimated coefficient for an independent variable X is b, when X is increased by one unit the logarithm of the outcome is expected to increase by b units. In terms of the outcome itself, its expected value is multiplied by e^b.

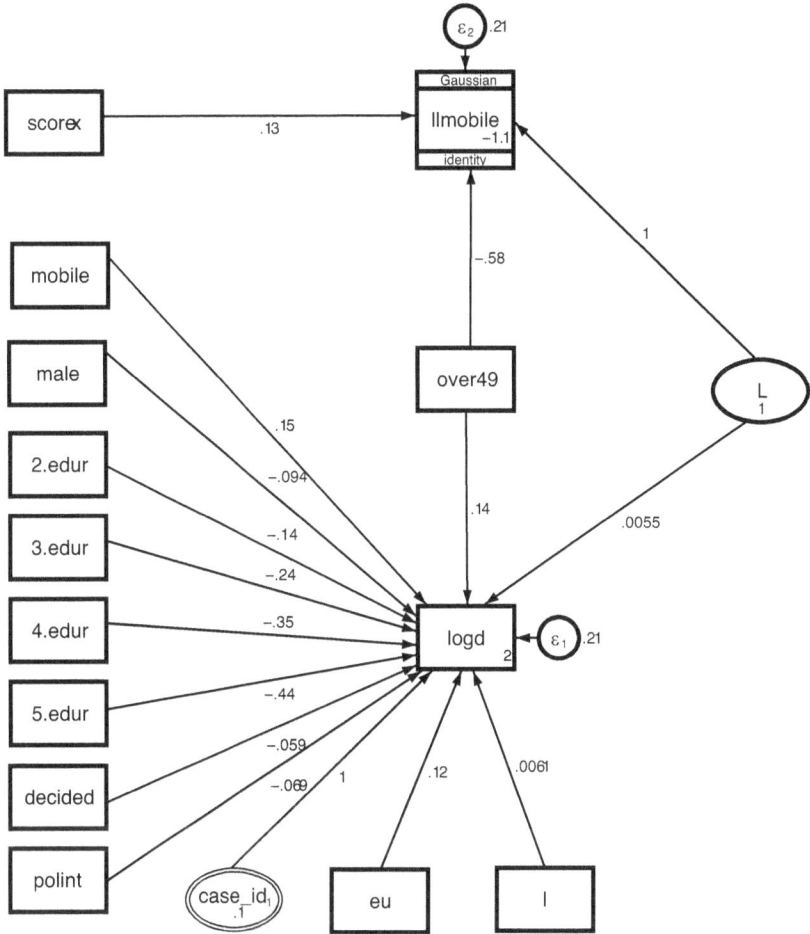

Figure 1: Generalized structural equation model.

	Coef	Std. Err.	z	P > z	[95% Conf Interval]	
ρ	0.011	0.140	0.08	0.937	−0.264	0.286

Table 1: Significance of the correlation.

According to **Figure 2**, the constant term is estimated at 2.01. This is the expected mean of the logarithm of the response times. According to **Table 2**, the exponential value of the constant term is 7.47. This is the geometric mean of response times.

In order to answer the main research question of this chapter, i.e. the impact of using a smartphone on the response time, I focus on the interpretation of

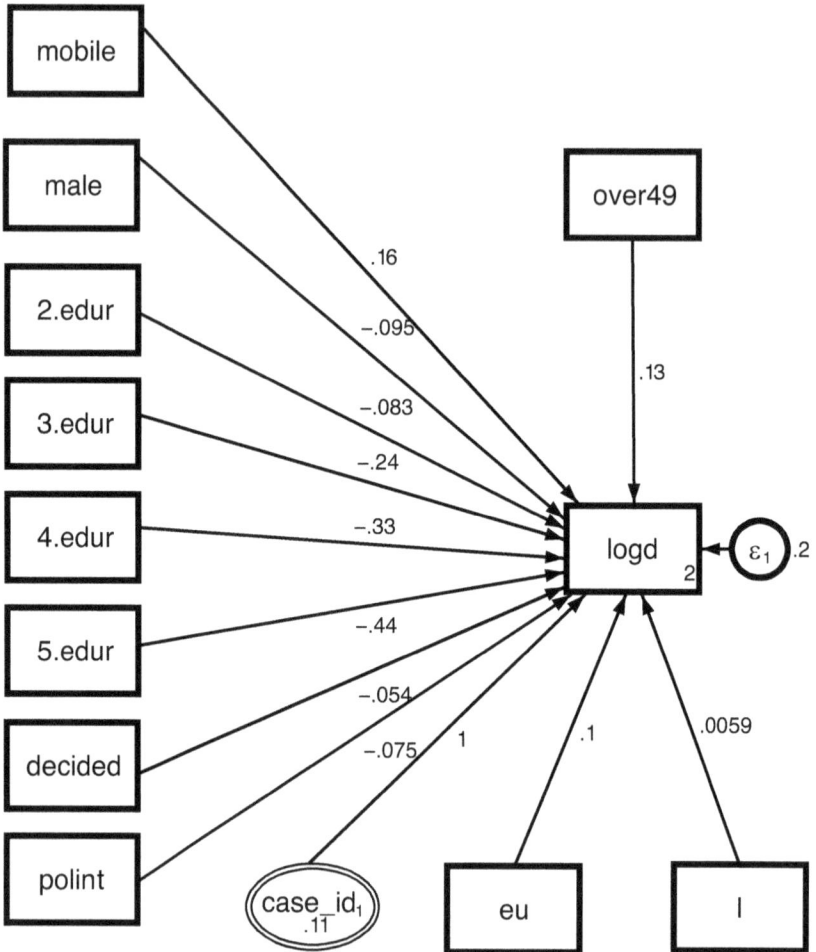

Figure 2: Generalized structural equation model equivalent to a multilevel linear regression model.

the coefficient of the mobile variable: the coefficient is 0.16 and the exponential value is 1.17. This means that when switching from desktop to smartphone the geometric mean of response times is expected to increase by 17%. To provide an estimate of the treatment effect in seconds, I calculate the increase on the overall geometric mean: 7.47*17% = 1.27 seconds per item. The impact on response times of using a mobile device is significant even after taking into account the impact of the control variables that were included in the model.

Moving on to the interpretation of the coefficients of the item characteristics, we can observe that the coefficient for the length of the statement (l) is 0.059 and its exponential value is 1.0059. This means that, while holding all other

Log of item response time	exp(b)	Std. Err.	z	P > z	[95% Conf.	Interval]
Mobile	1.175	0.015	12.43	0.000	1.145	1.205
Length of item (l)	1.006	0.000	111.77	0.000	1.006	1.006
EU issue (eu)	1.110	0.002	48.86	0.000	1.105	1.115
Male	0.909	0.009	−9.91	0.000	0.893	0.927
Over 49 years old (over49)	1.133	0.013	11.10	0.000	1.109	1.159
Vote choice (decided)	0.947	0.009	−5.94	0.000	0.930	0.964
Political interest (polint)	0.928	0.010	−7.29	0.000	0.909	0.947
Education (reference: Primary)						
Lower secondary (2.edu)	0.921	0.058	−1.30	0.193	0.813	1.043
Upper Secondary (3.edu)	0.784	0.043	−4.45	0.000	0.704	0.873
Tertiary (4.edu)	0.716	0.039	−6.15	0.000	0.644	0.797
Postgraduate studies (5.edu)	0.645	0.035	−8.02	0.000	0.579	0.718
M1[case_id]	2.718	.	.	.	.	.
Constant	7.471	0.412	36.48	0.000	6.706	8.323

Table 2: Generalized structural equation model equivalent to a multilevel linear regression model (exponentiated coefficients).

predictors constant, for every additional character in the statement the geometric mean of response times increases by 0.59%. According to the model, if a statement refers to an EU policy issue the respondents need more time to give their answer. The corresponding coefficient is 0.1 and its exponential value is 1.11, indicating an 11% increase in the geometric mean of response times when switching from a national issue to an EU issue.

Moving on to the user level, we can see that the coefficient for male is −0.095 and its exponential value is 0.909. This means that the geometric mean of response times in the group of men is 90.9% the geometric mean of response times in the group of women. In other words, switching from female to male respondents, the expected response time is decreased by 9.1%. Following the same logic, we observe that when we switch from undecided people to people who have already made their choice the geometric mean of response times is decreased by 5.3%. Similarly, moving from people who are not interested in politics to people who are interested in politics the geometric mean is expected to decrease by 7.2%. On the other hand, the exponentiated coefficient for older people is 1.13, indicating a 13% increase in the geometric mean of response times when switching from younger people to users over 49 years old. Finally, when we switch from primary education to higher education levels, the response time decreases; only the difference between primary and lower secondary education levels is not statistically significant. The largest difference is observed between the two extreme education levels: the ratio of geometric means of postgraduate studies to primary education levels is 0.64, indicating that the time spent by the most educated users is 64% the time spent by the less educated users, i.e. a decrease of 36%.

According to **Figure 2**, the variance of the random intercept is estimated to be 0.11 and the estimated error variance is 0.2. A likelihood ratio test indicates that the random intercept variance is large enough that we could not ignore it. This verifies that the decision to use a multilevel model was correct. Indeed, if a single level model had been used, non significant differences (e.g. the response time difference between primary and lower secondary education levels) would appear as significant.

Finally, I have explored whether there are any significant interaction terms between smartphone use and respondent characteristics (age, gender and education) or the length of the question. None of these interaction terms have a significant impact on the item response times at the 0.01 significance level.

Discussion

This chapter advances mobile research in various ways. Firstly, it offers a precise and thoroughly tested estimate of the impact of using a smartphone on item response times. The comparison was made between desktop and smartphone users when they use a voting advice application that was specifically designed to be used on smartphones. The analysis has shown that i) after taking into account item and user characteristics that are known to affect response times and ii) using the most suitable statistical models, when switching from desktop to smartphone the geometric mean of item response times is expected to increase by 17%.

The lack of a significant interaction between the use of a mobile device and the length of the question indicates that the longer times of smartphone users cannot be attributed to the smaller display of their devices. This finding was expected because the application was carefully designed to fit on the small screens of mobile devices. The lack of any significant interactions between smartphone use and respondent characteristics probably indicates that mobile users do not need more time because they face some difficulties while using their smartphones. If there was an issue of usability, this issue would probably be worse for older people. Thus, it seems that the most reasonable explanation for the longer times of smartphone users is that they are probably completing the survey outside of their home and their environment gives them more distractions than are available to the desktop users, who complete the survey in a more quiet room in their home or in their office.

In addition to the aforementioned finding, this chapter has presented an advanced statistical methodology to deal with the multilevel structure of the data while taking into account the endogeneity of the treatment. This is achieved by employing a generalized structural equation model that represents an endogenous treatment-effects multi-level regression. Although the data analysis performed in this chapter has shown that the correlation between the error terms was not significant and the simple multilevel model was adequate in this case, the advanced method proposed here may be necessary in other response time models with endogenous treatment variables.

Lastly, this chapter offers an innovative method to prepare a dataset of response times for statistical analysis by treating the low and the high extreme values differently. It shows how to flag users who have been answering so fast that they should be removed from the dataset. In addition, it proposes a way to deal with the extremely large response times by identifying the actual extremes instead of trimming the dataset using arbitrary selected threshold that lack any theoretical justification and lead to the removal of cases that should remain in the dataset.

I conclude this chapter with some ideas for further research on the topic. A more advanced model could compare three categories: desktop, smartphone and tablet users. Another extension could be to check the actual answers of the respondents for typical indicators of low quality (e.g. straight-lining) and try to test if there are any differences between mobile and desktop users. Other mobile/desktop comparisons could involve an analysis that would involve both response times and response patterns. In any case, since the trend shows a continuous increase of survey respondents using their mobile devices, the research community should focus on research projects that will help us build a deep understanding of the implications of this trend.

References

Andreadis, I. (2012). *To Clean or not to Clean?* Paper presented at the Improving the Quality of VAA Data XXII World Congress of Political Science (IPSA), Madrid, Spain. Retrieved from http://www.polres.gr/en/sites/default/files/IPSA12.pdf

Andreadis, I. (2013, September). *Voting Advice Applications: a successful nexus between informatics and political science.* Paper presented at BCI '13, Thessaloniki, Greece. DOI: http://doi.acm.org/10.1145/2490257.2490263

Andreadis, I. (2014a). Data Quality and Data Cleaning. In D. Garzia, & S. Marschall (Eds.), *Matching Voters with Parties and Candidates. Voting Advice Applications in Comparative Perspective.* ECPR Press. ISBN: 9781907301735

Andreadis, I. (2014b). *Paradata from Political Web Surveys.* Ann Arbor, MI: Inter-university Consortium for Political and Social Research [distributor]. Retrieved October 2, 2014. DOI: http://doi.org/10.3886/E17816V3

Bassili, J.N. and **Fletcher, J.F. (1991).** Response-time measurement in survey research a method for CATI and a new look at nonattitudes. *Public Opin.Q.,* *55*(3), 331–346.

Bauer, D. J. (2003). Estimating multilevel linear models as structural equation models. *Journal of Educational and Behavioral Statistics, 28*(2), 135–167. DOI: http://dx.doi.org/10.3102/10769986028002135

Carver, R.P. (1992) Reading rate: Theory, research, and practical implications. *Journal of Reading, 36*(2), 84–95

Couper, M. P, & **Kreuter, F.** (2013). Using Paradata to Explore Item Level Response Times in Surveys. *Journal of the Royal Statistical Society: Series A (Statistics in Society), 176*(1), 271–86. Wiley Online Library. DOI: http://dx.doi.org/10.1111/j.1467-985X.2012.01041.x

Couper, M. P, & **Peterson, G.** (2015). Exploring Why Mobile Web Surveys Take Longer. Paper presented at General Online Research 2015.

Curran, P. J. (2003). Have multilevel models been structural equation models all along? *Multivariate Behavioral Research, 38*(4), 529–569. DOI: http://dx.doi.org/10.1207/s15327906mbr3804_5

de Bruijne, M., & **Wijnant, A.** (2013). Comparing Survey Results Obtained via Mobile Devices and Computers: an Experiment with a Mobile Web Survey on a Heterogeneous Group of Mobile Devices Versus a Computer-Assisted Web Survey. Social Science Computer Review. Sage Publications, 0894439313483976. DOI: http://dx.doi.org/10.1177/0894439313483976

Fielding, R. T., Berners-Lee, T., & **Frystyk, H.** (1996). Hypertext Transfer Protocol--HTTP/1.0. Retrieved from http://tools.ietf.org/html/rfc1945

Fuchs, M., & **Busse, B.** (2009). The Coverage Bias of Mobile Web Surveys Across European Countries. *International Journal of Internet Science, 4*(1), 21–33.

Gelman, A., & **Hill, J.** (2006). Data analysis using regression and multilevel / hierarchical models. Cambridge: Cambridge University Press. DOI: http://dx.doi.org/10.1017/CBO9780511790942

Greene, W. H. (2012). Econometric Analysis. 7th ed. Upper Saddle River, NJ: Prentice Hall.

Gummer, T., & **Roßmann, J.** (2014). Explaining Interview Duration in Web Surveys a Multilevel Approach. Social Science Computer Review. SAGE Publications, 0894439314533479.

Heckman, J. (1978). Dummy endogenous variables in a simultaneous equation system. *Econometrica, 46,* 931–959. DOI: http://dx.doi.org/10.2307/1909757

Hoaglin, D.C., Mosteller, F., & **Tukey, J.W.** (1983). Understanding robust and exploratory data analysis. Wiley.

Hox, J. J. (2002). Multilevel analysis: Techniques and applications. Psychology Press.

Maddala, G. S. (1983). Limited-Dependent and Qualitative Variables in Econometrics. Cambridge: Cambridge University Press. DOI: http://dx.doi.org/10.1017/CBO9780511810176

Mavletova, A. (2013). Data Quality in PC and Mobile Web Surveys. Social Science Computer Review. Sage Publications, 0894439313485201. DOI: http://dx.doi.org/10.1177/0894439313485201

McGill, R., Tukey, J. W., & Larsen, W. A. (1978). Variations of box plots. *The American Statistician, 32,* 12–16.

Skrondal, A., & Rabe-Hesketh, S. (2004). Generalized latent variable modeling: Multilevel, longitudinal, and structural equation models. CRC Press. DOI: http://dx.doi.org/10.1201/9780203489437

Swanson, D. B., Case, S. M., Ripkey, D. R., Clauser, B. E., & Holtman M. C. (2001). Relationships among Item Characteristics, Examined Characteristics, and Response Times on USMLE Step 1. *Academic Medicine, 76*(10). DOI: http://dx.doi.org/10.1097/00001888-200110001-00038

Toepoel, V., & Lugtig, P. (2014). What Happens If You Offer a Mobile Option to Your Web Panel? Evidence from a Probability-Based Panel of Internet Users. Social Science Computer Review. SAGE Publications, 0894439313510482. DOI: http://dx.doi.org/10.1177/0894439313510482

Tourangeau, R., Rips, L. J., and Rasinski, K. (2000). The psychology of survey response. New York:

Tukey, J.W. (1977). Exploratory Data Analysis. Addison-Wesley.

van der Linden, W. J. (2008). Using Response Times for Item Selection in Adaptive Testing. *Journal of Educational and Behavioral Statistics, 33*(1), 5–20. DOI: http://dx.doi.org/10.3102/1076998607302626

Yan, T. and Tourangeau, R. (2008). Fast times and easy questions: The effects of age, experience and question complexity on web survey response times. *Applied Cognitive Psychology, 22*(1), 51-68

Wooldridge, J. M. (2010). Econometric Analysis of Cross Section and Panel Data. 2nd ed. Cambridge, MA: MIT Press.

CHAPTER 6

A Meta-Analysis of Breakoff Rates in Mobile Web Surveys

Aigul Mavletova* and Mick P. Couper[†]
*National Research University Higher School of Economics,
Russia, amavletova@hse.ru, [†]Institute for Social Research,
University of Michigan, USA

Abstract

In this chapter, we conduct a meta-analysis of breakoff rates in mobile web surveys. We test whether the optimization of web surveys for mobile devices, invitation mode (SMS vs. email), survey length, expected duration stated in the survey invitation, survey design (scrolling vs. paging), prerecruitment, number of reminders, design complexity (grids, drop-down questions, sliders, images, progress indicator), incentives, opportunity to skip survey questions, and opportunity to select the preferred mode (PC or mobile web) have an effect on breakoffs. The meta-analysis is based on 14 studies (39 independent samples) conducted using online panels – probability-based and non-probability-based. We found that mobile optimized surveys, email invitations, shorter surveys, using prerecruitment, more reminders, a less complex design, and an opportunity to choose the preferred survey mode all decrease breakoff rates in mobile web surveys. No effect of a scrolling design, incentives, indicating expected duration in the invitation, and letting an opportunity to skip survey questions was found.

Keywords

mobile web surveys, breakoff rates, meta-analysis

How to cite this book chapter:
Mavletova, A and Couper, M P. 2015. A Meta-Analysis of Breakoff Rates in Mobile Web Surveys. In: Toninelli, D, Pinter, R & de Pedraza, P (eds.) *Mobile Research Methods: Opportunities and Challenges of Mobile Research Methodologies*, Pp. 81–98. London: Ubiquity Press. DOI: http://dx.doi.org/10.5334/bar.f. License: CC-BY 4.0.

Introduction

Breakoff rates in mobile web surveys are a key challenge for survey researchers. The research software Kinesis Survey Technologies (2013) reports that mobile breakoff rates in the surveys hosted on their SaaS infrastructure varied from 68% to 84% in the period of 2012–2013. These breakoff rates appear to be increasing in 2013 compared to 2012. They are also significantly higher than those on PC, which vary from 17% to 23%. The overall percentage of mobile starts is 43% in 2013 (see Kinesis Survey Technologies 2013). The market research company Decipher reports about 20% of unintentional mobile respondents in their surveys and the average breakoff rate of 41% among smartphone respondents, compared to 24% among PC web respondents (Jue & Luck 2014). This is on average three million partial mobile web interviews per year. Lightspeed research reports about 10 million annual breakoffs in the US, and a growing percentage of mobile web respondents among them (Johnson, Kelly & Stevens 2012).

How can breakoff rates be decreased in mobile web surveys? In this chapter, based on a meta-analysis, we test if a variety of factors – including optimization of web surveys for mobile devices, invitation mode (SMS vs. email), survey length, indicating the expected duration of the survey in the invitation, survey design (scrolling vs. paging), prerecruitment, number of reminders, design complexity (grids, drop-down questions, sliders, images, progress indicator), incentives, an opportunity to skip survey questions, and an opportunity to select the preferred mode (PC or mobile web) – have an effect on breakoffs in mobile web surveys. The meta-analysis includes surveys conducted using online panels – both probability-based and non-probability-based volunteer panels.

Literature review and hypotheses

Galesic (2006) and Peytchev (2009) have explored the factors which can have an effect on breakoffs in PC web surveys. Peytchev (2009) found that presenting more questions on a single page and presenting questions with slider bars induce higher rates of breakoffs. Moreover, asking more burdensome questions, such as open-ended and long questions, as well as attitudinal questions, increased the likelihood of breakoffs on a page in PC web surveys. Galesic (2006) found that perceived interest and reported experienced burden can predict the likelihood of breakoffs in web surveys. Only a few experiments have measured factors which can affect breakoff rates in mobile web surveys (Mavletova & Couper 2014a; Mavletova & Couper 2014b). We have a number of expectations, based in part on these earlier experiments as well as on our assumptions.

The breakoff rates are higher in all types of mobile web surveys than in PC web surveys: this is the case for mobile-optimized (Baker-Prewitt 2013;

Buskirk & Andrus 2014; Lattery, Park Bartolone & Saunders 2013; Mavletova 2013; Mavletova & Couper 2013; Mavletova & Couper 2014a; Mavletova & Couper 2014b; Peterson et al. 2013), non-optimized (Bosnjak et al. 2013; Cunningham et al. 2013; Guidry 2012; Peterson 2012; Schmidt & Wenzel 2013), and mobile-app surveys (Wells, Bailey & Link 2013a; Wells, Bailey & Link 2013b). However, some experiments found lower breakoff rates in *mobile-optimized* than non-optimized web surveys among mobile users (Baker-Prewitt 2013; Peterson et al. 2013; Stapleton 2013; for exception see McGeeney & Marlar 2013). In the current meta-analysis, we expect to find that optimized mobile web surveys result in lower breakoff rates than non-optimized mobile web surveys.

Several papers have explored whether the *invitation mode* has an effect on breakoff rates in mobile web surveys. Maxl and his colleagues (2010) found that WAP (Wireless Application Protocol) push invitations, which display an alert invitation text on a mobile phone and direct respondents to a survey URL via a WAP browser, increased breakoff rates compared to SMS invitations, but resulted in similar participation rates. Mavletova and Couper (2014a) found that SMS invitations significantly increased both breakoff and participation rates relative to email invitations among mobile web respondents. Crawford and his colleagues (2013) also found that SMS slightly increased breakoff rates in a mobil-optimized web survey among students. We expect that email invitations decrease breakoff rates in mobile web surveys compared to SMS invitations.

Galesic and Bosnjak (2009) found that longer surveys produce higher breakoff rates in PC web surveys. Mavletova (2013) tested if *survey length* in mobile web surveys has an effect on breakoff rates. She compared surveys with expected durations of 5 and 15 minutes, which were completed on average within 10 and 29 minutes, respectively, and found slightly but not significantly higher breakoff rates in the longer survey. Pingatore and Seldin (2011) analyzed the location of breakoffs in a 100-item mobile web survey and found that most of the breakoffs occurred on the first screen – a pattern similar to PC web surveys. They suggest that survey length should not have a significant effect on breakoff rates in mobile web. Lattery, Park Bartolone, and Saunders (2013) found a larger effect of survey length on breakoff rates among mobile rather than PC web respondents in non-optimized surveys. We suggest that shorter surveys are associated with lower breakoff rates in mobile web surveys.

In addition, some surveys *include the estimated survey duration* in the invitation and some of them do not. We expect that indicating the survey duration decreases breakoff rates in mobile web surveys. When the expected survey duration is not mentioned in the invitation, the respondent's level of commitment may be lower, leading to a higher likelihood of breakoff, compared to when the survey duration is included (see Crawford, Couper & Lamias 2001; Yan et al. 2010).

Although the AAPOR task force on mobile technologies suggests minimizing the use of a *scrolling design* in mobile web surveys by limiting the number of questions displayed on a single page to a maximum of two (Link et al. 2014), some experiments show that a scrolling design in mobile web surveys decreases breakoff rates. McGeeney and Marlar (2013) compared different scrolling versions (1 and 3 pages) in 7-item and 13-item mobile-optimized and non-optimized web surveys with paging versions. They found lower breakoff rates in the scrolling versions in which all items were presented on a single page. Mavletova and Couper (2014a) found lower breakoff rates in a 17-item scrolling version of a mobile-optimized survey presented on two pages than in a paging version. Respondents were initially invited to complete the survey via a cell phone and the device noncompliance rate (completing the survey via PC) was 14%. However, the difference in breakoff rates between the paging and scrolling versions did not reach statistical significance ($\chi^2(1) = 3.365$, p = 0.067). In a subsequent experiment with a 30-item survey they compared different scrolling versions with 5, 15, or all 30 questions presented on a page in a survey with or without user-controlled skips (Mavletova & Couper 2014b). In the survey without skips the lowest breakoff rate was in the 30-item per page (scrolling) condition. However, the difference was not statistically significant ($\chi^2(2) = 3.611$, p = 0.164). No difference was found in the questionnaire with user-controlled skips. We expect that a scrolling design will produce lower breakoff rates than a paging design in mobile web surveys.

Some experiments conducted *prerecruitment surveys* to select those respondents who own cell phones with Internet access and who are willing to complete the main survey via a mobile device. Since even those respondents who own smartphones and use mobile Internet may not be willing to complete the survey via a mobile device, we suggest that using a prerecruitment survey decreases breakoff rates in mobile web surveys.

We also hypothesize that the *number of reminders* has an effect on breakoff rates. Reminders have an effect on response rates in PC web surveys (Brackbill et al. 2012; Cook, Heath & Thompson 2000). We suggest that sending reminders decrease breakoff rates in mobile web surveys.

We expect that some *survey design features* increase the complexity of a mobile web survey, in terms of both added download time and added effort required on the part of respondents. Such design elements as grids, drop-down questions, images, slider bars, and progress indicators can increase breakoff rates. Jue (2012) found a higher breakoff rate on grid questions among mobile respondents in non-optimized web surveys. Peterson and his colleagues (2013) found slightly but not significantly higher breakoff rates in a mobile-optimized web survey with drop-down menus and a survey with slider bars compared to a basic mobile-optimized web survey with a simple interface. Mavletova (2013) found that about a third of respondents were unable to see an image in a mobile-optimized web survey. Villar, Callegaro and Yang (2013), in their meta-analysis of breakoff rates in web surveys, found that using a constant progress indicator does not decrease breakoffs. Overall, we suggest that *less complex designs* produce lower breakoff rates in mobile web surveys.

Using *incentives* increases willingness to participate in web surveys (Göritz 2006). However, the effect depends on the size and type of incentives. Some researchers argue that incentives should be higher in mobile than PC web surveys to increase participation rates among mobile web users and compensate for additional survey burden. Wells, Bailey and Link (2013a; 2013b) offered mobile web respondents incentives that were five times higher than the usual incentives offered for completing a PC web survey. Johnson, Kelly and Stevens (2012) offered incentives for mobile web respondents that were three times higher than for PC web respondents in their experiment with a modular survey design. Buskirk and Andrus (2014) provided incentives for mobile web that were twice as high as that for a similar PC web survey. Due to experimental costs, Mavletova (2013) and Mavletova and Couper (2013; 2014a; 2014b) offered incentives for mobile web participation that were 40 percent lower than the usual incentives offered for PC web surveys in volunteer online panels. We expect that offering higher-than-usual incentives to panelists will decrease breakoff rates in mobile web surveys.

While we found no prior research on this topic, we also expect that an *opportunity to skip survey questions* and not answer all of them decreases survey burden. As a result, lower breakoff rates are expected compared to the condition where respondents are required to answer all questions.

Finally, we include two types of studies in the current meta-analysis – those studies which *assign respondents to the mobile web survey mode without giving respondents an opportunity to choose the device* (PC or mobile phone), and those studies which give participants an opportunity to select the preferred device. Assigning respondents to the mobile web survey mode means that respondents are explicitly asked to complete the survey via a mobile phone. We suggest that breakoff rates will be lower in the studies where respondents have a choice of device.

Methods

Literature search

Since research on mobile web surveys has only recently emerged and a number of studies have not (yet) been published, we included both published studies and unpublished conference presentations in our meta-analysis. We used the web survey methodology bibliographic database (http://www.websm.org) and searched for relevant papers from conferences such as those held by the AAPOR, General Online Research (GOR), European Survey Research Association (ESRA), ESOMAR, from the CASRO online research and digital research conferences, and from WebDataNet and the MESS (Measurement and Experimentation in the Social Sciences) workshops. The keywords used for searching were: 'mobile web', 'smartphone web', 'mobile web surveys', and 'smartphone web surveys'. We did not focus on tablet-only surveys; however, most of the papers included tablet users in the definition of mobile web users.

Inclusion criteria

A study was included in the meta-analysis if it met the following criteria: (1) it was conducted using online panels – both probability and non-probability-based; (2) respondents could either be assigned to mobile web surveys without having an opportunity to choose the device or be able to select their pre-ferred device (PC web or mobile web); (3) mobile web surveys could be either browser-based or app-based; and (4) the study reported relevant statistics on breakoff rates and moderators. The search and inclusion criteria resulted in the inclusion of 14 studies with 39 independent samples (see a brief description of the studies and samples in **Table 1**).

Moderators

We included the moderators discussed in the hypotheses and literature review section in the model. Additionally, we planned to include such variables as the country of data collection, the average number of items presented on a page, the panel type (probability or non-probability), and the year of data collection. However, due to higher multicollinearity (VIF more than 15) these variables were excluded from the meta-analysis. The other moderators included in the model had a VIF lower than 5, except for survey length. Survey length had a VIF of 5.6. Socio-demographic variables were not included in the current meta-analysis, since not all experiments reported this information.

№	Study	Breakoff Rates (mobile devices only)
1	Baker-Prewitt 2013	13% in a mobile optimized survey, 18% in a non-optimized survey
2	Buskirk & Andrus 2014	30.9% in a mobile optimized survey
3	de Bruijne & Wijnant 2013	5.5% in a mobile optimized survey
4	Lattery, Park Bartolone & Saunders 2013	20.9% in a mobile optimized survey
5	Mavletova 2013	16.3% in a shorter survey, 20.3% in a longer survey
6	Mavletova & Couper 2013	13.6% in the first wave, 12.7% in the second wave

№	Study	Breakoff Rates (mobile devices only)
7	Mavletova & Couper 2014a	11.5% in the paging design in SMS invitation, 10.4% in the scrolling design in SMS invitation, 7.5% in the paging design in email invitation, 3.1% in the scrolling design in email invitation
8	Mavletova & Couper 2014b	12.2% in the scrolling design with one page, 13.0% in the scrolling design chunked into two pages, 14.9% in the scrolling design chunked into three pages
9	McGeeney & Marlar 2013[25]	2.7% in a non-optimized 13-item survey with a scrolling design chunked into three pages, 1.0% in a non-optimized 7-item survey with a paging design, 1.4% in a non-optimized 13-item survey with a paging design, 0.9% in a non-optimized 7-item survey with a scrolling design with one page, 0.9% in an optimized 13-item survey with a scrolling design chunked into three pages, 0.4% in an optimized 7-item survey with a paging design, 2.4% in an optimized 13-item survey with a paging design, 1.4% in a non-optimized 13-item survey with a scrolling design with one page, 0.5% in an optimized 13-item survey with a scrolling design with one page
10	Pearson 2012	22.2% in a mobile optimized web survey
11	Peterson et al. 2013	13% in a non-optimized mobile web survey, 5% in an optimized mobile web survey, 4% in an optimized mobile web survey with numeric input, 7% in an optimized mobile web survey with sliders, 5% in an optimized mobile web survey with drop-down questions
12	Stapleton 2013	8.2% in a longer mobile optimized web survey with progress indicator, 10.2% in a longer mobile optimized web survey with progress indicator and drop-down questions, 6.3% in a shorter mobile optimized web survey with progress indicator, 7.8% in a shorter mobile optimized web survey with progress indicator and drop-down questions, 15.9% in a non-optimized web survey
13	Toepoel & Lugtig 2014	1.4% in a mobile optimized web survey
14	Wells, Bailey & Link 2013b	3.7% in a mobile-app survey, 5.3% in a in a non-optimized web survey

Table 1: Description of the Studies.

[25] A non-optimized 7-item web survey with a scrolling design with one page is not included in the analysis, since no breakoffs were found in that condition.

Moderators were included using the following code: mobile-optimized web survey = 1 and non-optimized web survey = 0; email invitation = 1 and SMS invitation = 0; survey length varying from 2 to 30 minutes; expected duration is included in the invitation = 1, expected duration is not included = 0; scrolling design = 1, paging design = 0; prerecruitment = 1, no prerecruitment = 0; number of reminders varying from 0 to 2; survey design complexity varying from 0.2 = one out five design elements to 1 = all five elements (grids, drop-down questions, images, slider bars, and progress indicator); incentives varying from 0 = no incentives to 5 = incentives five times higher than typical incentives for PC web surveys; survey questions obligatory to complete = 1 and respondents have an opportunity to skip some questions = 0; and surveys assigned respondents to mobile web mode = 1 and respondents could select the preferred mode = 0.

Sample characteristics

The current meta-analysis includes 39 independent samples, with the breakoff rates varying from 0.9% to 30.9% and with a total number of 4,209 breakoffs among 34,589 participants who started the surveys. On average, 2.6% of participants were tablet users. About two thirds of the surveys are from the United States (65%), 28% are from Russia, and 7% from European countries. The surveys were conducted between 2010 and 2013. More than a half (54%) of the studies assigned respondents to a mobile web survey without giving them an opportunity to select their preferred mode. Despite this, some respondents completed the survey in the PC web survey mode in these latter experimental studies. Breakoff rates were calculated based only on mobile web respondents in our meta-analysis. About a third of the surveys were conducted using probability-based panels.

Meta-analytic procedure

Since breakoff rates (BR) are calculated as the proportion of those who broke off out of all those who started the survey, the proportions can be used as the effect size. Lipsey and Wilson (2001) suggest that using proportions less than 0.20 underestimates the confidence intervals of mean proportions and overestimates the heterogeneity of the proportions across surveys. Almost all breakoff rates in the current meta-analysis are lower than 0.20. In that case the proportion is transformed into log transformed proportion: $ln\left(\dfrac{BR}{1-BR}\right)$. The effect sizes are reported in log transformed proportions and odds ratios (OR, see **Table 2**). We used the 'metafor' package – a meta-analysis package in R – for data analysis (http://www.metafor-project.org; Chen & Peace 2013).

Results

Influential case diagnostics (Viechtbauer 2010; Viechtbauer & Cheung 2010) show that three surveys are influential outliers, since the Cook's distances, standardized residuals, and DFFITS values of these surveys are large. To reduce the impact of these studies (Buskirk & Andrus 2014; Pearson 2012; Wells, Bailey & Link 2013b) we truncated the effect size to the upper or lower bound of the 90% confidence interval of the effect size calculated without these outliers (see Gnambs 2013). There was also an outlier in the sample size (a non-optimized web survey in Stapleton 2013). We truncated it to the largest sample size of the remaining surveys.

A random-effects model of breakoff rates shows that the average breakoff rate in mobile web surveys is 6.6% with the confidence interval of 5.3% to 8.2% (see log transformed proportions in forest plot in **Figure 1**). The test for heterogeneity ($Q(38) = 628.78$, $p < 0.001$) is statistically significant, which means that the studies included in the analysis are heterogeneous. The percentage of total variation due to variation between studies is very high ($I^2 = 97.7\%$). 95% confidence interval in brackets.

A mixed-effects meta-regression explains the $R^2 = 0.86$ of the random between-study variance (τ^2). As expected, mobile-optimized surveys, email invitations, shorter surveys, using prerecruitment, a larger number of reminders, a less complex design, and an opportunity to choose the preferred survey mode (PC web or mobile web) are significantly associated with lower breakoff rates in mobile web surveys (see **Table 2**).

Mobile-optimized web surveys decrease the odds of breakoffs among mobile respondents by 0.71 ($p < 0.01$, see **Table 2**) compared to non-optimized web surveys. Email invitations decrease the odds of breakoffs by 0.47 ($p < 0.001$) compared to SMS invitations. Prerecruitment decreases the odds of breakoffs by 0.68 ($p < 0.05$). Sending a larger number of reminders also decreases the odds of breakoffs ($p < 0.01$). Sending one reminder decreases the odds of breakoffs by 0.85, two reminders by 0.54, and three reminders by 0.39 compared to sending only the invitation. Including such design elements as grids, drop-down questions, images, slider bars, and progress indicators increases the probability of breakoffs ($p < 0.001$). Including one complex design element increases the odds of breakoffs by 1.30, and including all five elements by 1.91, compared to the condition without any of these elements. If respondents have an opportunity to select their preferred mode the odds of breakoff rates are decreased by 0.62 ($p < 0.05$) compared to the surveys in which respondents are initially assigned to a mobile web survey mode. Survey length did not reach statistical significance ($p = 0.07$). However, it explains the largest proportion of the between-study variance ($R^2 = 0.45$). A 10-minute survey increases the odds of breakoffs by 1.09 and a 30-minute survey by 1.42 compared to a 5-minute mobile web survey.

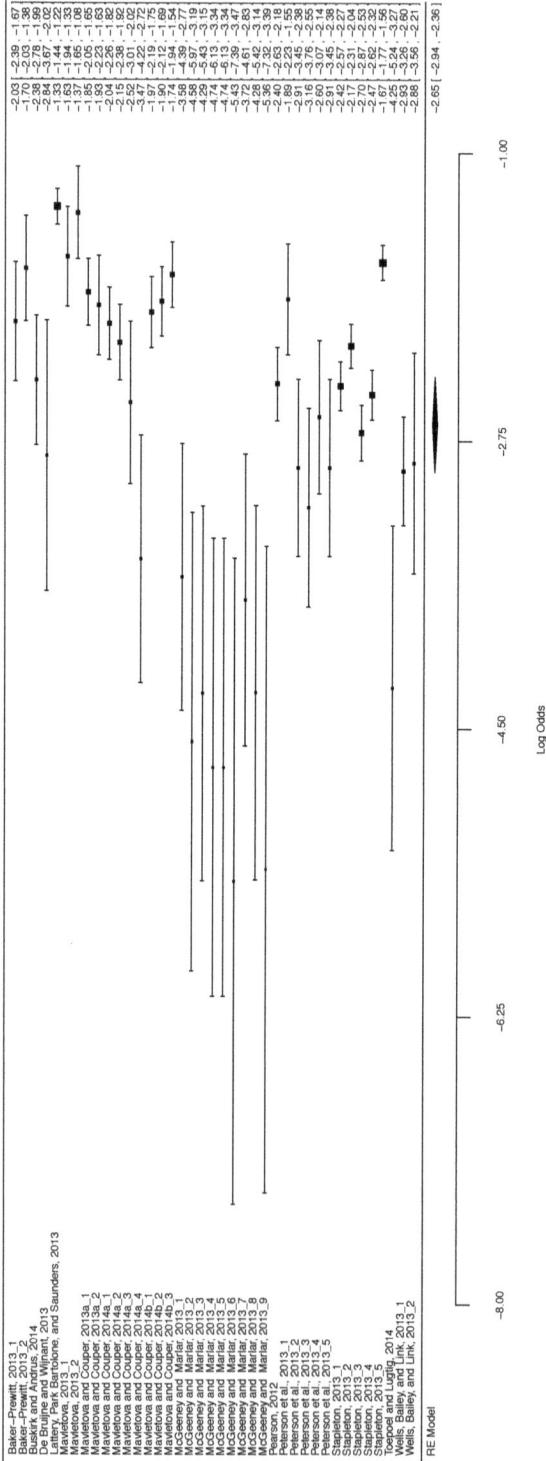

Baker–Prewitt, 2013_1	-2.03 [-2.39 , -1.67]
Baker–Prewitt, 2013_2	-1.70 [-2.03 , -1.38]
Buskirk and Andrus, 2014	-2.38 [-2.78 , -1.99]
De Bruijne and Wijnant, 2013	-2.84 [-3.67 , -2.02]
Lattery, Park Bartolone, and Saunders, 2013	-1.33 [-1.44 , -1.22]
Mavletova, 2013_1	-1.63 [-1.94 , -1.33]
Mavletova, 2013_2	-1.37 [-1.65 , -1.08]
Mavletova and Couper, 2013a_1	-1.85 [-2.05 , -1.65]
Mavletova and Couper, 2013a_2	-1.93 [-2.23 , -1.63]
Mavletova and Couper, 2014a_1	-2.04 [-2.26 , -1.82]
Mavletova and Couper, 2014a_2	-2.15 [-2.38 , -1.92]
Mavletova and Couper, 2014a_3	-2.52 [-3.01 , -2.02]
Mavletova and Couper, 2014a_4	-3.47 [-4.22 , -2.72]
Mavletova and Couper, 2014b_1	-1.97 [-2.19 , -1.75]
Mavletova and Couper, 2014b_2	-1.90 [-2.12 , -1.69]
Mavletova and Couper, 2014b_3	-1.74 [-1.94 , -1.54]
McGeeney and Marlar, 2013_1	-3.58 [-4.39 , -2.77]
McGeeney and Marlar, 2013_2	-4.58 [-5.97 , -3.19]
McGeeney and Marlar, 2013_3	-4.29 [-5.43 , -3.15]
McGeeney and Marlar, 2013_4	-4.74 [-6.13 , -3.34]
McGeeney and Marlar, 2013_5	-4.74 [-6.13 , -3.34]
McGeeney and Marlar, 2013_6	-5.43 [-7.39 , -3.47]
McGeeney and Marlar, 2013_7	-3.72 [-4.61 , -2.83]
McGeeney and Marlar, 2013_8	-4.28 [-5.43 , -3.14]
McGeeney and Marlar, 2013_9	-5.36 [-7.32 , -3.39]
Pearson, 2012	-2.40 [-2.63 , -2.18]
Peterson et al., 2013_1	-1.89 [-2.45 , -1.55]
Peterson et al., 2013_2	-2.91 [-3.45 , -2.38]
Peterson et al., 2013_3	-3.16 [-3.76 , -2.55]
Peterson et al., 2013_4	-2.60 [-3.07 , -2.14]
Peterson et al., 2013_5	-2.91 [-3.45 , -2.38]
Stapleton, 2013_1	-2.42 [-2.57 , -2.27]
Stapleton, 2013_2	-2.17 [-2.31 , -2.04]
Stapleton, 2013_3	-2.70 [-2.87 , -2.53]
Stapleton, 2013_4	-2.47 [-2.62 , -2.32]
Stapleton, 2013_5	-1.67 [-1.77 , -1.56]
Toepoel and Lugtig, 2014	-4.25 [-5.24 , -3.27]
Wells, Bailey, and Link, 2013_1	-2.93 [-3.26 , -2.60]
Wells, Bailey, and Link, 2013_2	-2.88 [-3.56 , -2.21]
RE Model	-2.65 [-2.94 , -2.36]

Figure 1: Forest Plot: Breakoff Rates (Log Transformed Proportions).

Factors	Lower breakoff rates in mobile web surveys are expected:	Supported/ not supported	Effect size: log transformed proportions and the odds ratios
Optimization for mobile devices	in optimized mobile web surveys	supported	$ln\left(\dfrac{BR}{1-BR}\right) = -0.60$ ∗∗ (−0.98, −0.21) OR = 0.71 (0.54, 0.89)
Invitation mode	in email than in SMS invitation	supported	$ln\left(\dfrac{BR}{1-BR}\right) = -1.18$ ∗∗∗ (−1.70, −0.67) OR = 0.47 (0.31, 0.68)
Survey length	in shorter surveys	supported (p = 0.07)	$ln\left(\dfrac{BR}{1-BR}\right) = 0.04$ (0.00, 0.09)+ OR (10 to 5 min) = 1.09 (0.99, 1.16) OR (20 to 5 minutes) = 1.27 (0.97, 1.40) OR (30 to 5 minutes) = 1.42 (0.95, 1.53)
Including expected survey duration in the invitation	in surveys which include the expected duration in the invitation	not supported	$ln\left(\dfrac{BR}{1-BR}\right) = -0.38$ (−1.08, 0.32) n.s.
Survey design	in a scrolling than in a paging design	not supported	$ln\left(\dfrac{BR}{1-BR}\right) = -0.12$ (−0.61, 0.37) n.s.
Prerecruitment	in surveys with a prerecruitment phase	supported	$ln\left(\dfrac{BR}{1-BR}\right) = -0.67$ ∗ (−1.20, −0.14) OR = 0.68 (0.46, 0.93)

(Continued)

Factors	Lower breakoff rates in mobile web surveys are expected:	Supported/ not supported	Effect size: log transformed proportions and the odds ratios
Number of reminders	in surveys with a larger number of reminders	supported	$ln\left(\dfrac{BR}{1-BR}\right) = -0.31$ ** (−0.53, −0.09) OR (1 to 0 reminders) = 0.85 (0.74, 0.96) OR (2 to 0 reminders) = 0.54 (0.35, 0.84) OR (3 to 0 reminders) = 0.39 (0.20, 0.77)
Survey design complexity (grids, drop-down questions, images, slider bars, and progress indicators)	in surveys with a lower design complexity	supported	$ln\left(\dfrac{BR}{1-BR}\right) = 3.06$ *** OR (1 to 0 elements) = 1.30 (1.20, 1.39) OR (5 to 0 elements) = 1.91 (1.76, 1.97)
Incentives	in surveys with higher incentives	not supported	$ln\left(\dfrac{BR}{1-BR}\right) = 0.11$ (−0.10, 0.32) n.s.
Opportunity to skip survey questions	in surveys with an opportunity to skip survey questions	not supported	$ln\left(\dfrac{BR}{1-BR}\right) = 0.14$ (0.53, 0.64) n.s.
Assigned to mobile web or could choose the mode	in surveys with an opportunity to select the preferred mode (PC web or mobile web)	supported	$ln\left(\dfrac{BR}{1-BR}\right) = -0.81$ * (−1.55, −0.06) OR = 0.62 (0.35, 0.97)

Table 2: Hypotheses and Effect Sizes.

***p < 0.001, **p < 0.01, *p < 0.05, + p = 0.07; 95% confidence interval in parentheses

No effect of a scrolling design, incentives, indicating the expected duration of the survey in the invitation, and an opportunity to skip survey questions was found.

Discussion and conclusion

What are the implications of the meta-analysis presented here? It shows the importance of optimizing web surveys for mobile devices to minimize breakoffs among mobile respondents. While this might be self-evident, using less complex design elements should also be considered. Using such elements as grids, sliders, and images is associated with higher breakoffs among mobile respondents. Shorter surveys are more efficient. There is research evidence that completing a survey on a smartphone takes more time than completing a survey on a PC (de Bruijne & Wijnant 2013; Gummer & Roßmann 2014; Mavletova 2013; Mavletova & Couper 2013; Pearson 2012; Peterson et al. 2013; Wells, Bailey & Link 2013a). One possible solution for mobile web surveys can be to use modular (or chunked) surveys. Johnson, Kelly and Stevens (2012) proposed using app-based modular surveys, which chunk a long web survey into shorter 5–10-minute surveys for mobile respondents. They found that while the breakoff rates in a full PC web survey was 6%, all mobile respondents who started completing the modules in a mobile application finished all five modules. Moreover, there was a lower perceived survey burden among mobile than PC web respondents in terms of the subjective evaluation of the survey length (more respondents stated that the survey was shorter than expected). However, in their following experiment Kelly, Johnson and Stevens (2013) found slightly higher breakoff rates in a modular mobile survey than in a PC web survey. Siluk, Johnson and Tarraf (2013) also found higher breakoff rates in a modular mobile web survey (25%) than in a full mobile (8%) or in a full PC web survey (11%). It is worth including modular mobile web surveys in a future meta-analysis to measure whether it decreases breakoff rates compared to a full mobile web survey.

We found that sending a larger number of reminders, using prerecruitment, giving an opportunity for respondents to select the preferred mode (vs. assignment to mobile web survey mode), and sending email (vs. SMS) invitations are associated with lower breakoff rates in mobile web surveys. There is some research evidence, however, that SMS invitations increase participation rates among mobile web respondents compared to PC web respondents (Crawford et al. 2013; Mavletova & Couper 2014a).

Contrary to expectations, no effect of the scrolling design was found. This can be due to limitations in the current meta-analysis. Only three studies included in the current analysis (Mavletova & Couper 2014a; Mavletova & Couper 2014b; McGeeney & Marlar 2013) tested scrolling versions. McGeeney and Marlar (2013) had a small number of mobile respondents in their survey, with only a few breakoffs in each of the scrolling and paging versions. Mavletova and Couper (2014a; 2014b) found slightly (but not significantly) lower breakoff rates for the scrolling design in two studies. To measure the effect of this design feature in future meta-analyses, it is worth including a larger number of experiments and measuring odds ratios of breakoff rates between the scrolling and paging designs in mobile web surveys.

We found no effect of higher incentives on breakoff rates in mobile web surveys. Despite these results we still suggest that higher incentives can both increase participation rates and decrease breakoff rates in mobile web surveys. However, to our knowledge, no experiments comparing the effect of different incentives have been conducted among mobile web samples.

The current meta-analysis of breakoff rates in mobile web surveys should be considered as preliminary. It is based on two types of studies, those which assign respondents to mobile web mode and those in which respondents could select the mode they prefer. Since there is a self-selection bias in the latter studies, future meta-analyses should be restricted, as a sufficient number of studies become available, to those studies which randomly assign respondents to a PC or mobile web mode. The current analysis did not measure the effect of app-based versus mobile-browser-based surveys on breakoff rates, since only 1 study among the 14 had an app-based condition (Wells, Bailey & Link 2013b). We hypothesize that app-based mobile surveys may have lower breakoff rates because there is no need for a persistent Internet connection. However, they may have higher nonresponse rates, because of the need to install the app. In a future meta-analysis, it is worth comparing these two types of surveys. We also did not measure the single effect of different design elements (grids, drop-down questions, sliders, images, progress indicators) on breakoff rates. In a future meta-analysis it is worth exploring the effect of each survey element and taking into consideration more details for each, such as the number of grids, sliders, and images in the survey, the number of items in the grids, etc. Due to higher multicollinearity, such variables as the country of data collection, number of survey items presented on a single page, panel type (probability or non-probability), and year of data collection were not included in the analysis. We suggest that these variables could also have explained some proportion of the random between-study variance. Though the survey length explained the largest proportion of the between-study variance, it did not reach statistical significance ($p = 0.07$). This could be due to higher multicollinearity. In a future meta-analysis which would include a larger number of studies, we would expect to find effects of survey length on breakoff rates.

In spite of these limitations, the current meta-analysis shows that researchers should take into consideration some basic survey features such as mobile optimization, survey length, and questionnaire design elements while designing surveys for both PC and mobile web respondents. These design elements have an effect on breakoffs (as we have shown here), but also on measurement error (as several papers have shown, e.g., McClain & Crawford 2013; Peterson et. al. 2013).

Acknowledgement of funding sources

This work was supported by the research grant [13-05-0035] provided to the first author under 'The National Research University Higher School of Economics Academic Fund Program' in 2013–2014.

References

Baker-Prewitt, J. (2013, March). *Mobile research risk: What happens to data quality when respondents use a mobile device for a survey designed for a PC.* Paper presented at the CASRO Online Research Conference, San Francisco, USA.*

Brackbill, R., Yu, S., Walker, D., Turner, L., Miller, S., Farfel, M., & Stellman, S. (2012, May). *Multiple email reminders and response rate for an internet based survey.* Paper presented at the AAPOR Annual Conference, Orlando, FL, USA.

Buskirk, T.D., & Andrus, C. (2014). Making mobile browser surveys smarter: results from a randomized experiment comparing online surveys completed via computer or smartphone. *Field Methods*, published online before print 14 April 2014. DOI: http://dx.doi.org/10.1177/1525822X14526146*

Chen, D.-G., & Peace, K.E. (2013). Applied meta-analysis. Boca Raton, FL: R. Taylor & Francis Group.

Cook, C., Heath, F., & Thompson, R.L. (2000). A meta-analysis of response rates in web- or internet-based surveys. *Educational and Psychological Measurement, 60*(6), 821–836. DOI: http://dx.doi.org/10.1177/00131640021970934

Crawford, S.D., Couper, M.P., & Lamias, M.J. (2001). Web surveys. Perceptions of burden. *Social Science Computer Review, 19*(2), 146–162. DOI: http://dx.doi.org/10.1177/089443930101900202

Crawford, S. D., McClain, C. A., O'Brien, S., & Nelson, T. F. (2013, May). *Examining the feasibility of SMS as a contact mode for a college student survey.* Paper presented at the AAPOR Annual Conference, Boston, USA.

de Bruijne, M., & Wijnant, A. (2013). Comparing survey results obtained via mobile devices and computers: An experiment with a mobile web survey on a heterogeneous group of mobile devices versus a computer-assisted web survey. *Social Science Computer Review, 31*(4), 482–504. DOI: http://dx.doi.org/10.1177/0894439313483976*

Galesic, M. (2006). Dropouts on the web: Effects of interest and burden experienced during an online survey. *Journal of Official Statistics, 22*(2), 313–328.

Galesic, M., & Bosnjak, M. (2009). Effects of questionnaire length on participation and indicators of response quality in a web survey. *Public Opinion Quarterly, 73*, 349–360. DOI: http://dx.doi.org/10.1093/poq/nfp031

Gnambs, T. (2013). The elusive general factor of personality: The acquaintance effect. *European Journal of Personality, 27*, 507–520. DOI: http://dx.doi.org/10.1002/per.1933

Göritz, A. S. (2006). Incentives in web studies: Methodological issues and a review. *International Journal of Internet Science, 1*(1), 58–70.

Gummer, T., & Roßmann, J. (2014). Explaining interview duration in web surveys: A multilevel approach. *Social Science Computer Review*, published online 21 May 2014. DOI: http://dx.doi.org/10.1177/0894439314533479

Johnson, A., Kelly, F., & Stevens, S. (2012, March). *Modular survey design for mobile devices.* Paper presented at the CASRO Online Research Conference, Las Vegas, USA.

Jue, A. (2012). Participation of mobile users in traditional online studies. White paper. Fresno, CA: Decipher.

Jue, A., & Luck, K. (2014). *Update: Participation of mobile users in online surveys.* Decipher White Paper. Retrieved from https://www.decipherinc.com/n/uploads/images/pages/Decipher_Mobile_Research_White_Paper_Update.pdf.

Kelly, F., Johnson, A., & Stevens, S. (2013, March). *'Bite-sized chunks'- mobile and CAWI parallel proposal.* Paper presented at the Online Research Conference, San-Francisco, USA.

Kinesis Survey Technologies. (2013). *Kinesis Whitepaper – Online Survey Statistics from the Mobile Future.* Retrieved from http://www.kinesissurvey.com/wp-content/uploads/2013/10/UPDATED-with-Q3-2013-Data-Mobile-whitepaper.pdf

Lattery, K., Park Bartolone, G., & Saunders, T. (2013, March). *Optimizing surveys for smartphones: Maximizing response rates while minimizing bias.* Paper presented at the CASRO Online Research Conference, San Francisco, USA.*

Link, M. W., Murphy, J., Schober, M. F., Buskirk,T. D., Hunter Childs, J., & Tesfaye, C. L. (2014). *Mobile technologies for conducting, augmenting and potentially replacing surveys: Report of the AAPOR task force on emerging technologies in public opinion research.* Retrieved from http://www.aapor.org/Mobile_Technologies_Task_Force_Report.htm. DOI: http://dx.doi.org/10.1093/poq/nfu054

Lipsey, M. W., & Wilson, D. B. (2001). Practical meta-analysis. Thousand Oaks, CA: Sage.

Mavletova, A. (2013). Data quality in PC and mobile web surveys. *Social Science Computer Review, 31*(6), 725–743. DOI: http://dx.doi.org/10.1177/0894439313485201*

Mavletova, A., & Couper, M.P. (2013). Sensitive topics in PC web and mobile web surveys. *Survey Research Methods, 7*(3), 191–205.*

Mavletova, A., & Couper, M. P. (2014a). Mobile web survey design: Scrolling versus paging, SMS versus e-mail invitations. *Journal of Survey Statistics and Methodology, 2*(4), 498–518. DOI: http://dx.doi.org/10.1093/jssam/smu015*

Mavletova, A., & Couper, M.P. (2014b). Grouping of items in mobile web questionnaires. *Field Methods*, forthcoming.*

Maxl, E., Haring, W., Tarkus, A., Altenstrasser, M., & Dolinar, M. (2010). Effects of mobile web survey invitation modes on non-response. *International Journal of Mobile Marketing, 5*(1), 5–14.

McClain, C., & Crawford, S. D. (2013, May). *Grid formats, data quality, and mobile device use: A questionnaire design approach.* Paper presented at the AAPOR Annual Conference, Boston, USA.

McGeeney, K., & Marlar, J. (2013, May). *Mobile browser web surveys: Testing response rates, data quality, and best practices.* Paper presented at the AAPOR Annual Conference, Boston, USA.*

Pearson, C. (2012, May). *Devices used to access surveys are changing rapidly - are you prepared?* Paper presented at the CASRO Technology Conference, New York, USA.*

Peterson, G., Mechling, J., LaFrance, J., Swinehart, J., & Ham, G. (2013, March). *Solving the unintentional mobile challenge.* Paper presented at the CASRO Online Research Conference, San Francisco, USA.*

Peytchev, A. (2009). Survey breakoff. *Public Opinion Quarterly, 73*(1), 74–97. DOI: http://dx.doi.org/10.1093/poq/nfp014

Pingatore, G., & Seldin, D. (2011). Five things about mobile data collection. ESOMAR. Retrieved from http://rwconnect.esomar.org/5-things-about-mobile-data-collection

Siluk, L., Johnson, E. P., & Tarraf, S. (2013, March). *Cyborgs vs. monsters: Assembling modular surveys to create complete datasets.* Paper presented at the Online Research Conference, San Francisco, USA.

Stapleton, C.E. (2013). The smartphone way to collect survey data. *Survey Practice, 6*(2).*

Toepoel, V., & Lugtig, P. (2014). What happens if you offer a mobile option to your web panel? Evidence from a probability-based panel of internet users. *Social Science Computer Review, 32*(4), 544–560. DOI: http://dx.doi.org/10.1177/0894439313510482*

Viechtbauer, W. (2010). Conducting meta-analyses in R with the metaphor package. *Journal of Statistical Software, 36*(3). Retrieved from http://cran.r-project.org/web/packages/metafor/vignettes/metafor.pdf

Viechtbauer, W., & Cheung, W. (2010). Outlier and influencer diagnostics for meta-analysis. *Research Synthesis Methods, 1*, 110–125. DOI: http://dx.doi.org/10.1002/jrsm.11

Villar, A., Callegaro, M., & Yang, Y. (2013). Where am I? A meta-analysis of experiments on the effects of progress indicators for web surveys. *Social Science Computer Review, 31*(6), 744–762. DOI: http://dx.doi.org/10.1177/0894439313497468

Wells, T., Bailey, J., & Link, M. W. (2013a). Comparison of smartphone and online computer survey administration. *Social Science Computer Review, 32*(2), 238–255. DOI: http://dx.doi.org/10.1177/0894439313505829

Wells, T., Bailey, J., & Link, M. W. (2013b). Filling the void: gaining a better understanding of tablet-based surveys. *Survey Practice, 6*(1).*

Yan T., Conrad, F. G., Tourangeau, R., & **Couper, M. P.** (2010). Should I stay or should I go: The effects of progress feedback, promised task duration, and length of questionnaire on completing web surveys. *International Journal of Public Opinion Research, 23*(2), 131–147. DOI: http://dx.doi.org/10.1093/ijpor/edq046

* Article included in the meta-analysis.

CHAPTER 7

Who Are the Internet Users, Mobile Internet Users, and Mobile-Mostly Internet Users?: Demographic Differences across Internet-Use Subgroups in the U.S.

Christopher Antoun

Institute for Social Research, Ann Arbor, USA,
antoun@umich.edu

Abstract

Survey researchers must now decide which data collection device or mix of devices is optimal for their Web survey (e.g., whether they will permit computers only or permit smartphones only). Their choice has implications for who can be observed and who cannot be observed. Yet there has been little research about the population subgroups that might be absent from different of types of Web surveys. This chapter takes a step in the direction of such research by exploring demographic differences across various subgroups of Internet users using data from a national telephone survey conducted in the US. Four overlapping groups are considered: the general population; those who go online using a computer; those who go online using a phone; and those who go online using mostly a phone, as opposed to other devices. In a novel approach to simplify the study of these groups, the process of using the Internet is modeled as a series of three transitions from one group to the next. This analysis sheds light on whether the effects of demographic characteristics are the same for each transition to a different level of Internet use. I also explore differences between these Internet use subgroups with respect to non-demographic survey variables after controlling for demographic differences.

How to cite this book chapter:
Antoun, C. 2015. Who Are the Internet Users, Mobile Internet Users, and Mobile-Mostly Internet Users?: Demographic Differences across Internet-Use Subgroups in the U.S.. In: Toninelli, D, Pinter, R & de Pedraza, P (eds.) *Mobile Research Methods: Opportunities and Challenges of Mobile Research Methodologies*, Pp. 99–117. London: Ubiquity Press. DOI: http://dx.doi.org/10.5334/bar.g. License: CC-BY 4.0.

Keywords

Web surveys, Internet access, mobile Web surveys, mobile Web access, mobile-mostly users

Introduction

The rise of mobile devices is changing the way that people go online. People are increasingly using their mobile devices to complete online tasks that were once reserved for personal computers or laptops (e.g., checking email, reading the news, online shopping, or social networking). In addition, an increasing percentage of mobile users go online mostly using their mobile devices as opposed to their computers (Duggan & Smith 2013).

For online survey researchers, this change presents both opportunities and challenges. The opportunities are mostly related to survey measurement. Smartphones provide ways to enhance measurement through the use of apps (e.g., survey apps, diary apps that prompt respondents) and other smartphone features (e.g., GPS, camera, Bluetooth-enabled sensors) (see AAPOR 2014). The challenges, on the other hand, have to do with reaching people in the general population and with the differences between those who are reached and those who are not reached. In the past, when personal computers were virtually the only way to access the Internet, Web coverage was only a function of the difference between those who went online using a computer and those who did not go online at all. However, the rapid rise of Internet-enabled personal devices has created other groups of Internet users, all of which have implications for coverage in online surveys. For example, if a traditional Web survey omits mobile phone users (by blocking them or using a non-optimized survey), then their absence from the sample might affect the accuracy of estimates based on Web surveys (Antoun & Couper 2013). Mobile surveys might also affect coverage. If a mobile-only survey omits computer users (because it uses an app or takes advantage of the advanced features of smartphones), then their absence from the sample might bias estimates based on mobile-only surveys (Fuchs & Busse 2009). The picture becomes more complicated when other devices, like tablets (not to mention e-readers, gaming consoles, etc.) are considered, and will no doubt become even more complex with the devices of the future (e.g., watches, wearable glasses, etc.).

Unfortunately, there has been little research about the characteristics of these different subgroups of Internet users, even though such knowledge might be informative for survey researchers who are grappling with which data collection device or mix of devices to use in order to reach the most people and who seek to understand which demographic groups may be underrepresented in their particular type of online survey (e.g., one that permit computers only, an app that permits smartphones only, or a hybrid or adaptive design approach that accommodates all devices). While some studies have estimated coverage error in surveys designed for computers (e.g., Mohorko, de Leeuw & Hox 2013) and in surveys designed for mobile devices (e.g., Fuchs & Busse 2009), this chapter takes a different approach. Using data from a Pew US national telephone survey, I explore demographic differences across various subgroups of Internet users. I distinguish between four overlapping groups: 1) the general population; 2) those who go online using a computer; 3) those who go online using a phone; and 4) those who go online mostly using a phone as opposed to other devices. Here I use the term 'go online' to refer not only to *access* but also to at least occasional *use* of a particular device to connect to the Internet. While there is also a small percentage of people who *only* use a phone but not a computer to go online, they make up such a small minority of US Internet users that they are not considered here (i.e., all phone users considered in this chapter also use a computer to go online). Tablets are not considered either, because the characteristics of their users do not have coverage implications for online surveys designed for mobile phones or computers; since tablets are not the focus of this chapter, from here on out I use the term 'mobile' to refer only to mobile phones.

As shown in **Figure 1**, when using the above classification the four groups are concentric in that each subsequent group is fully contained within the previous one(s). By definition, a member of group 4 (mobile-mostly user) is also a member of groups 3, 2, and 1 (mobile user; computer user; general population); a member of group 3 (mobile user) is also a member of groups 2 and 1 (computer user; general population) but not necessarily group 4 (mobile-mostly user).

Because membership in a group is conditional on membership in the previous one(s), it is possible to conceptualize these as stages from which one can make up to three transitions, starting in group 1 and moving as far as group 4: that is, 1) an individual can transition from never going online to going online using a computer; 2) conditional on computer Internet use, they also have the opportunity to transition to going online using a phone; and 3) conditional to mobile Internet use, they can also transition to going online using mostly a phone. Each of these transitions represents movement from one side of a digital gap to the other side: one bridges a digital divide by starting to go online using a computer, a device divide by starting to go online using a phone, and what I call a *usage* divide (in the sense that they begin to use their phone more than other devices) by starting to go online using mostly a phone.

It should be noted that my focus is on Internet use in the US, where there has been a rapid shift in online use that matches these transitions. This framework would be less appropriate in other settings, such as developing countries, where a large proportion of people skipped the first transition altogether and started going online using a phone without ever having regularly used a computer (e.g., see Poushter, Bell & Oates 2015).

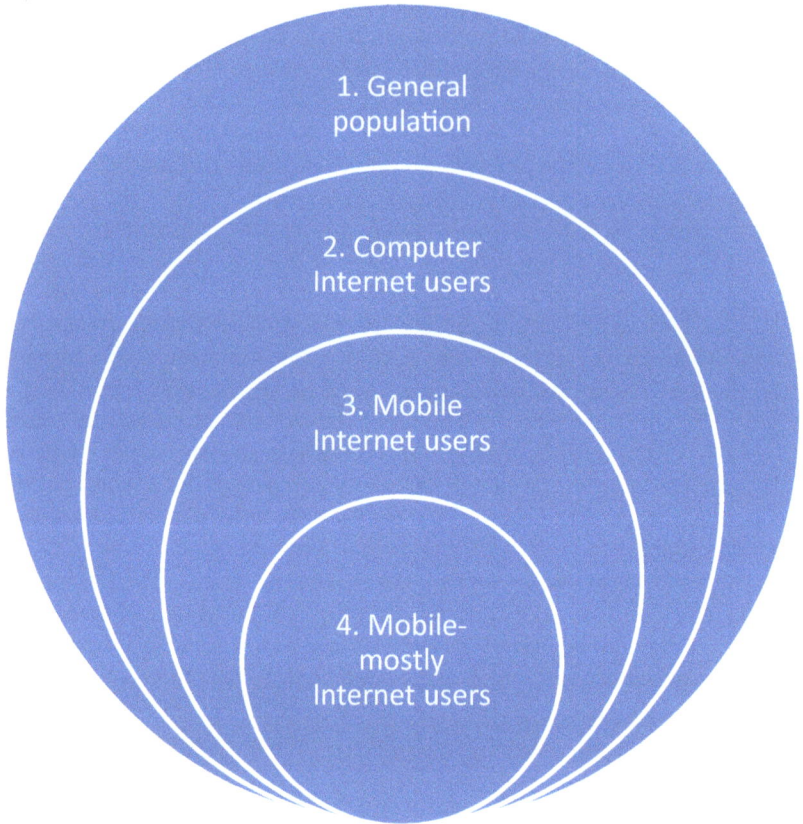

Figure 1: Internet Use Subgroups. Note: Figure not drawn to scale.

Conceptualizing Internet use in this way raises several questions about the effect of demographic characteristics at each transition. For example, age is known to play a role in Internet adoption, but does it also drive the transitions to going online using a phone and going online using mostly a phone? As for education, does its initial effect diminish with the transition to using a phone to go online or to using mostly a phone to go online? Race is also known to affect Internet adoption, but in what way, if any, is it also associated with the other two transitions? The primary objective of this chapter, therefore, is to investigate whether the effect of demographic characteristics are the same for each of these three transitions to a different level of Internet use. A secondary objective of this chapter is to investigate whether, conditional on the demographic variables, there is a relationship between substantive survey variables and these different levels of Internet use. The results will have implications for whether the omission of certain population subgroups in Web surveys might affect the accuracy of these surveys.

The Three Digital Divides

As mentioned earlier, each of the three transitions under study in this chapter represents a kind of movement from one side of a digital gap to the other side. In this section, these three divides – the digital divide, device divide, and *usage* divide – are described in more detail.

Digital divide

Much attention has been paid to the distinction between those who go online and those who do not, i.e., the digital divide (Lenhart 2003). This was a concern as far back as 1995 (NTIA 1995), when a privileged group of only 3% of US residents had ever used the Internet (Pew 1995). Since then Internet use in the US has grown steadily and is now estimated to be as high as 85% (Zickuhr 2013). But there is evidence that a gap still exists between Internet users and non-users. According to recent analyses of US survey data, Internet access decreases with age and increases with education, and non-Hispanic Black and Hispanic people are more likely to have access to the Internet than White people (Bethlehem 2010; Tourangeau, Conrad & Couper 2013). For online survey practitioners, uneven Internet use across population groups has implications for coverage errors, because those on one side of the divide differ from those on the other side with regard to survey variables of interest such as health ratings and voting behavior (Bethlehem 2010; Couper et al. 2007; Dever, Rafferty & Valliant 2008; Mohorko, de Leeuw & Hox 2013).

Device divide

While the digital divide is still present, another type of divide has emerged, the so-called 'device divide' (Pearce & Rice 2013). This divide makes a distinction between those who go online using their phones and those who go online but not using their phone. The number of mobile Internet users varies widely by country and region but appears to be growing in almost all places (for a more detailed overview, see Revilla et al. 2014). Just in the past few years, the percentage of mobile Internet users has recorded notable growth and is now estimated to be at 43% in Europe (Eurobarometer data retrieved from Metzler & Fuchs 2014) and 55% in the US (Duggan & Smith 2013). But as with the digital divide, there is evidence that those on one side of the device divide differ from those on the other side. Using US national telephone surveys, Smith (2012) reports that mobile Internet users are younger, better educated, and more likely to be Black or Hispanic compared to those who do not use the mobile Internet. Using a face-to-face survey conducted in 33 European countries (Eurobarometer), Fuchs and Busse (2009) report similar differences: mobile Internet users are younger, more likely to be male, and more likely to be single. The extent of the differences for non-demographics variables is still unclear.

Usage divide

Finally, a *usage* divide between those who go online mostly using their phones and those who go online mostly using their computers is emerging among mobile Internet users. This transition has been highlighted in several recent reports produced by survey organizations (e.g., Duggan & Smith 2013; Smith 2012; Townsend & Rios 2011). It occurs when an individual begins to forgo using their computer in favor of their phone. For multi-device users, the choice of device for online activities might depend on several factors such as the complexity and length of the task (Robinson 2014), the time of day (Lipsman & Aquino 2013), or whether they are at home or at work. With this in mind, it may be difficult for respondents to report their general go-to device for online browsing; nonetheless, when asked to do so they increasingly report choosing their phones. In just the past few years, the percentage of mobile-mostly users in the US has nearly doubled, jumping from 8% in 2011 to 15% in 2013 (Duggan & Smith 2013). Users who prefer to use mobile phones for online tasks may be especially likely to take online surveys using their phone (de Bruijne & Wijnant 2014), whether mobile use was intended by the designers of the survey or not (Peterson 2012). Of course, mobile-centric status does not mean that one cannot complete a survey using other devices – users can still make an exception and answer a survey on a computer. As with the other two divides, there is some evidence of differences between those on either side of the division. Duggan and Smith (2013) report that young adults, non-Whites, the less well educated, and the less affluent are more likely to go online using mostly their phones rather than other devices. This is perhaps a reflection of high-education individuals wanting to complete more complicated online tasks (e.g., banking, graphic design, and so forth) on a computer, and not on a phone (Robinson 2014). Little is known, however, about the differences between mobile-mostly Internet users and computer-mostly Internet users on non-demographic survey variables.

This chapter will explore demographic differences not only within each one of these three divides, but also across them. Given the evidence that technology use is generally higher among younger, highly educated, and more affluent persons, I expect to find several consistent effects across the three divides, including: an age effect – Internet use declines with age; an education effect – Internet use increases with education; and an income effect – Internet use increases with income. As mentioned earlier, I will also test for differences between these groups with regards to survey variables of interest (after controlling for demographic differences), because any significant differences could have coverage error implications for Web surveys.

Methods

Data were analyzed from one year (2012) of the Pew Internet and American Life Project's Spring Tracking Study. This was a project of the Pew Research Center, a nonpartisan think tank based in Washington, DC. The study consisted of a US national telephone survey of adults aged 18 and older that used a dual-frame landline and cellular random digit dial (RDD) sample. Interviews were conducted in English and Spanish. The questionnaire contained approximately 60 questions, mostly on the topic of technology use. Data collection was carried out by Princeton Survey Research Associates International. There were 2,254 completed interviews (1,351 landline and 903 cell) and the response rate was 11%. The low response rate can be partially attributed to the larger trend of declining response rates in US telephone surveys (Curtin, Presser & Singer 2005). While higher response rates are desirable, this low response rate is not necessarily an indicator of nonresponse bias in the estimates (Groves & Peytcheva 2008), especially since the topic of the survey (i.e., technology use) was not made explicit in the introduction that was read by interviewers. To know about Internet users and non-users, one needs data on both groups, and an interviewer-administered survey allows for this in a way that a Web survey does not. Of course, there is the chance of coverage error in the estimates based on telephone surveys because people without phones were excluded, but they are estimated to make up a relative small proportion (about 2%) of the US population (Blumberg & Luke 2013). To help reduce these potential biases and make inferences to the general US population of adults (aged 18 and older), all analyses presented here were weighted using the combined first-stage weights (to account for overlapping sample frames and different household sizes) and second-stage poststratification weights (see Duggan & Rainie 2012 for information about the estimation of weights).

In my analysis, I used the following demographics variables: age (18–24 versus 25–34, 35–44, 45–54, 55–64, or 65 and older); education (less than high school graduate versus high school graduate, some college/Associate's degree, or college graduate or more); income (less than US$30,000 versus US$30,000–US$75,000, more than US$75,000, or don't know/refused); gender (male versus female); and race/ethnicity (White/not Hispanic versus, Black/not Hispanic, Hispanic, or other). These variables were chosen because they are used for poststratification weighting by Pew and because they are commonly used to describe differences between adults with and without Internet access. I also used the following three non-demographic survey variables: quality of life (excellent/very good/good versus fair/poor/don't know/refused); social trust ('most people can be trusted' versus 'you can't be too careful'/'it depends'/don't know/refusal); tablet user ('yes' versus 'no'/don't know/refusal). These variables serve as examples of substantive variables that might be measured using a Web survey. I chose these three items because they are of substantive interest to Pew, and because they were administered to all respondents, regardless of whether or not they have Internet (some items in the survey were not administered to non-Internet users).

There are a number of different ways to measure how people go online, and consideration can be given to access versus use, individual use versus household use, location of use, and so forth. As mentioned earlier, I focus not on access only but on at least occasional use of a particular device to connect to the Internet. I defined Internet use at the individual level and not the household level. Also, I did not consider the places where people use the Internet, even though some people's online time may be concentrated at work or at home (or at the library or a coffee shop for that matter). In my analysis, an individual who goes online using a computer is someone who answered 'yes' to either of two questions – 'Do you use the internet, at least occasionally?' or 'Do you send or receive email, at least occasionally?' – and who reported owning either a 'desktop computer' or a 'laptop computer'. An individual who goes online using a phone is someone who answered 'yes' to either of these questions: 'Do you ever use your cell phone to send or receive email?' or 'Do you ever use your cell phone to access the internet?' As noted earlier, all phone users considered in this analysis also use a computer to go online (the small number of people (n = 69 or 3.1% of the sample) who *only* use a phone but not a computer to go online are excluded). The excluded mobile-only respondents did not differ reliably from the mobile-mostly respondents in terms of gender or race/ethnicity, but they were slightly older than the mobile-mostly respondents. Finally, an individual who goes online using mostly a phone is someone who answered 'mostly on a cell phone' rather than 'mostly on something else', 'both equally', 'depends', or 'don't know' to the following question: 'Overall, when you use the internet, do you do that mostly using your cell phone or mostly using some other device like a desktop, laptop or tablet computer?'

Statistical analysis

As mentioned earlier, I consider four overlapping groups of Internet users. I take advantage of the fact that membership in one group is conditional on membership in the previous one(s), and I model the process of gaining Internet access as a series of binary choices by fitting three sequential logistic regression models that are estimated by conditioning on the appropriate subsamples of the data. For model 1, I used the full sample (n = 2254) to model computer Internet use vs. non-use. In this group, 74.1% of respondents report going online using a computer (75.2% in the weighted analysis). For model 2, I condition on computer Internet use (n = 1671) and then model mobile Internet use vs. non-use (i.e., the conditional probability of going online using a phone). In this subsample, 61.0% of respondents report going online using a phone (66.9% in the weighted analysis). For model 3, I condition on mobile Internet use (n = 1019) and model mobile-mostly use vs. computer-mostly use (i.e., the conditional probability of going online using mostly a phone). In this subsample, 16.4% of respondents report going online using mostly a phone (21.1% in the weighted analysis).

Results

For this analysis, I first fit the multivariate models using only demographic variables. The results will shed light on demographic differences between users and non-users at each level of Internet use. They will also reveal whether the effects of demographic characteristics are the same for each of the three transitions to a different level of Internet use. I then refit the models using both demographics variables and non-demographics variables to see if the additional variables are associated with being a particular type of Internet user over and above the demographic predictors.

Demographics-only models

The series of conditional logic models and their odds ratios are presented in **Table 1**. Model 1 reveals that all five demographic variables were significantly associated with computer Internet use. Such users are younger, more likely to be female, better educated, more likely to be White than Black or Hispanic, and more affluent than non-users. I examined the bivariate relationships of these variables to find that, for age, computer Internet use decreased in a monotonic way from 87.9% among those respondents aged 18–24 to 50.6% among those aged 65 and older. Computer Internet use increased monotonically with education from 43.1% among those with less than a high school degree to 92.2% among college graduates.

Model 2 reveals that (conditional on computer Internet use), mobile Internet users are younger, better educated, and more likely to be Black or Hispanic than White, and more affluent than mobile Internet non-users. As with computer Internet use, mobile Internet use decreased with age from 77.9% among those respondents aged 18–24 to 19.4% among those aged 65 and older, but it increased with education from 42.5% among those with less than a high school degree to 67.2% among college graduates. Mobile Internet use among Black and Hispanic respondents (64.2% and 63.5%, respectively) was higher than among White respondents (52.7%).

Model 3 reveals that (conditional on mobile Internet use), mobile-mostly Internet users are younger, and more likely to be Black than computer-mostly Internet users. As with the other types of Internet use, mobile-mostly use decreased with age from 26.6% among those respondents aged 18–24 to less than 2% for each of the two oldest age groups (55–64 and 65 and older). Mobile-mostly Internet use increased with education up to a point, from 8.2%

Predictor	Model 1: Computer Internet Use			Model 2: Mobile Internet Use Given Computer Internet Use			Model 3: Mobile Mostly Internet Use Given Mobile Internet Use		
	Odds ratio	95% CI	p value	Odds ratio	95% CI	p value	Odds ratio	95% CI	p value
Age			< 0.001			< 0.001			< 0.001
18–24	–	–		–	–		–	–	
25–34	0.39	(0.21, 0.73)		0.95	(0.57, 1.59)		0.86	(0.54, 1.38)	
35–44	0.31	(0.16, 0.56)		0.53	(0.33, 0.86)		0.43	(0.26, 0.72)	
45–54	0.23	(0.13, 0.39)		0.27	(0.173, 0.42)		0.17	(0.09, 0.32)	
55–64	0.13	(0.07, 0.21)		0.10	(0.07, 0.16)		0.02	(0.01, 0.08)	
65+	0.07	(0.04, 0.11)		0.06	(0.04, 0.09)		0.04	(0.01, 0.13)	
Education			< 0.001			< 0.001			0.009
Less than HS graduate	–	–		–	–		–	–	
HS graduate	2.31	(1.52, 3.53)		1.41	(0.92, 2.17)		1.38	(0.70, 2.75)	
Some College/Assoc Degree	4.68	(3.01, 7.28)		1.90	(1.22, 2.95)		2.39	(1.23, 4.66)	
College Graduate	9.66	(5.93, 15.75)		2.82	(1.80, 4.41)		1.28	(0.63, 2.58)	
Income			< 0.001			< 0.001			0.232
Less than $30,000	–	–		–	–		–	–	

	OR	(95% CI)	p	OR	(95% CI)	p	OR	(95% CI)	p
$30,000 – $75,000	3.98	(2.78, 5.69)		1.29	(0.94, 1.79)		1.26	(0.78, 2.05)	
More than $75,000	6.85	(4.05, 11.61)		2.95	(2.03, 4.27)		1.59	(0.92, 2.75)	
Don't know/refused	1.28	(0.90, 1.82)		1.21	(0.86, 1.71)		0.89	(0.48, 1.65)	
Gender (male)	0.71	(0.54, 0.94)	0.018	0.99	(0.79, 1.25)	0.960	0.88	(0.62, 1.26)	0.489
Race/Ethnicity			< 0.001			0.002			< 0.001
White/not Hispanic	—	—		—	—		—	—	
Black/not Hispanic	0.50	(0.33, 0.77)		1.80	(1.26, 2.59)		2.84	(1.78, 4.56)	
Hispanic	0.46	(0.30, 0.72)		1.73	(1.15, 2.59)		1.34	(0.79, 2.26)	
Other	1.01	(0.55, 1.85)		1.12	(0.67, 1.89)		0.99	(0.49, 1.99)	
Unweighted n	2254			2254			2254		
$X^2(15)$	2249.00			2079.04			962.89		
R^2	0.63			0.60			0.35		
Max-rescaled R^2	0.65			0.61			0.39		

Table 1: The Odds Ratios Representing the Effect of Demographic Factors on Internet Use.

among those with less than a high school degree to 17.9% among those with some college/associates degree, but then declined among college graduates (9.4%). Mobile-mostly Internet use among Black respondents was 23.5% compared to only 9.3% among White respondents.

The explanatory power of the demographic factors declines from an R^2 of 0.63 in Model 1, to 0.60 in Model 2, to finally 0.35 in Model 3. This suggests that demographics variables have more explanatory power when predicting computer Internet use and mobile Internet use than mobile-mostly Internet use, perhaps because other factors like familiarity with technology are more predictive of mobile-mostly Internet use.

Do demographic characteristics have the same effect for each of these three transitions to a different level of Internet use?

The expected age effect – Internet use declines with age – is the only effect that is consistent across all levels of Internet use. For example, compared to the youngest age group (18–24), being in the oldest age group (65 and older) reduces the odds of being a computer Internet user by 93%; it similarly reduces the odds of being a mobile Internet user (conditional on computer Internet use) by 94%; and it reduces the odds of being a mobile-mostly Internet user (conditional on mobile Internet use) by 96%.

The expected education effect – Internet use increases with education – is not monotonic across all levels of Internet use. Compared to the lowest education group (less than high school degree), being in the highest education group (college degree) increases the odds of being a computer Internet user by a factor of 9.7; it increases the odds of being a mobile Internet user (conditional on computer Internet use) by a factor of 2.8; however, it has no significant effect on the odds of being a mobile-mostly Internet user (conditional on mobile Internet use). Similarly, the expected income effect – Internet use increases with income – is not monotonic across all levels of Internet use. Being in the highest income group has a positive effect on computer Internet use and mobile Internet use (Models 1 and 2), but it had no effect on becoming a mobile-mostly user (Model 3). This suggests that high-education and high-income adults make the transition to having Internet and make the transition to going online using their phones, but they stop short of relying on their phones to go online.

Gender was only associated with computer Internet use (Model 1), and not with the other two transitions. Race/ethnicity was the only characteristic that had the opposite effect on the first transition (computer Internet use) compared to the other two transitions (mobile Internet use and mobile-mostly Internet use). Non-Hispanic Black and Hispanic respondents are less likely to make the first transition to going online using a computer (Model 1), but conditional on Internet access they are more likely to make the second transition to using their phones to go online (Model 2), and conditional on mobile Internet use, Black respondents are more likely to make the final transition to use mostly a phone to go online (Model 3).

Adding substantive variables

The demographic differences between users and non-users reported above can lead to errors of nonobservation in surveys. However, these differences can be accounted for by standard weighting procedures. Therefore, the important issue is whether there are differences between users and non-users on non-demographic variables, and whether these differences persist after controlling for demographic differences.

Next, I fit a series of binary logit models, one for each level of Internet use, but this time I add to the baseline demographics model a series of three non-demographic variables (indicators of quality of life, social trust, and tablet ownership). **Table 2** shows the odds ratios for each variable. As before, I conditioned on the appropriate subsamples of the data for each model. Since the baseline models from **Table 1** are nested in these new models, I am able to conduct likelihood ratio tests. The log likelihood ratio test-statistic, which is Chi-square distributed (with three degrees of freedom), is shown in the last row of **Table 2**.

For Model 1, the likelihood ratio test reveals that the addition of the non-demographic variables adds significantly to the model, over and above the demographic controls ($X^2(3) = 200.9$, $p < 0.001$). Tablet use was significantly associated with Internet use; computer Internet users are 5.6 times more likely to use a tablet compared to computer Internet non-users.

For Model 2, the addition of the non-demographic variables also adds significantly to the model ($X^2(3) = 587.7$, $p < 0.001$). As with Model 1, this new model reveals that of the three predictors only tablet use is significantly associated with mobile Internet use, but it produces a relatively strong effect: mobile Internet users are 9.2 times more likely to use a tablet compared to non-users of mobile Internet.

For Model 3, once again the non-demographic variables add significantly to the model ($X^2(3) = 53.8$, $p < 0.001$). And once again tablet use was the lone significant predictor; mobile-mostly Internet users are 1.8 times more likely to use a tablet compared to computer-mostly Internet users.

I used a rather limited set of five demographic controls. But when I added to the model a larger set of demographic variables (marital status, employment status, regions, and urbanicity), tablet use was still significantly associated with each of the levels of Internet use. These results suggest that coverage error may affect the accuracy of at least some estimates based on online surveys designed for computers. For example, if traditional Web surveys disproportionately omit mobile-mostly users (by blocking them or using a non-optimized survey), then

Predictor	Model 1: Computer Internet Use			Model 2: Mobile Internet Use Given Computer Internet Use			Model 3: Mobile Mostly Internet Use Given Mobile Internet Use		
	Odds ratio	95% CI	p value	Odds ratio	95% CI	p value	Odds ratio	95% CI	p value
Age			< 0.001			< 0.001			< 0.001
18–24	–	–		–	–		–	–	
25–34	0.41	(0.21, 0.80)		1.02	(0.60, 1.72)		0.85	(0.52, 1.37)	
35–44	0.36	(0.19, 0.67)		0.58	(0.36, 0.94)		0.43	(0.25, 0.74)	
45–54	0.26	(0.15, 0.47)		0.29	(0.18, 0.46)		0.18	(0.010, 0.33)	
55–64	0.16	(0.09, 0.28)		0.11	(0.07, 0.18)		0.03	(0.01, 0.08)	
65+	0.08	(0.05, 0.14)		0.07	(0.04, 0.10)		0.04	(0.01, 0.15)	
Education			< 0.001			0.001			0.008
Less than HS graduate	–	–		–	–		–	–	
HS graduate	2.24	(1.46, 3.45)		1.32	(0.85, 2.04)		1.42	(0.71, 2.84)	
Some College/Assoc Degree	4.41	(2.80, 6.95)		1.72	(1.09, 2.72)		2.45	(1.25, 4.82)	
College Graduate	8.15	(4.92, 13.50)		2.26	(1.41, 3.61)		1.31	(0.63, 2.71)	
Income			< 0.001			0.001			0.405
Less than $30,000	–	–		–	–		–	–	
$30,000 – $75,000	3.54	(2.46, 5.10)		1.09	(0.77, 1.53)		1.18	(0.72, 1.94)	

	Model 1 OR	95% CI	p	Model 2 OR	95% CI	p	Model 3 OR	95% CI	p
More than $75,000	5.13	(2.99, 8.80)		1.99	(1.34, 2.96)		1.39	(0.77, 2.49)	
Don't know/refused	1.11	(0.77, 1.60)		1.02	(0.71, 1.46)		0.82	(0.45, 1.51)	
Gender (male)	0.70	(0.52, 0.94)	0.016	0.98	(0.77, 1.25)	0.871	0.90	(0.62, 1.29)	0.548
Race/Ethnicity			< 0.001			0.003			< 0.001
White/not Hispanic	–	–		–	–		–	–	
Black/not Hispanic	0.52	(0.33, 0.80)		1.91	(1.31, 2.79)		2.72	(1.68, 4.42)	
Hispanic	0.42	(0.26, 0.66)		1.60	(1.04, 2.46)		1.22	(0.72, 2.05)	
Other	1.11	(0.60, 2.04)		1.20	(0.69, 2.09)		0.98	(0.49, 1.98)	
Quality of Life (good)	1.28	(0.92, 1.77)	0.140	1.14	(0.83, 1.55)	0.421	1.17	(0.68, 2.03)	0.576
Social trust (high)	1.30	(0.94, 1.81)	0.112	1.24	(0.95, 1.61)	0.115	0.71	(0.47, 1.08)	0.107
Use tablet (yes)	5.61	(2.75, 11.46)	< 0.001	9.22	(6.18, 13.76)	< 0.001	1.77	(1.16, 2.68)	0.008
Unweighted n	2254			2254			2254		
$X^2(18)$	2449.87			2666.77			1016.67		
R^2	0.66			0.69			0.36		
Max-rescaled R^2	0.68			0.70			0.40		

Table 2: The Odds Ratios Representing the Effect of Demographic Factors and Non-Demographic Factors on Internet Use.

their absence from the sample has the potential to affect some estimates based on Web surveys (e.g., estimates of tablet use).

Discussion

This chapter offered a new way to conceptualize Internet use as a series of three transitions, each involving a jump from one side to the other side of a digital divide. It reported on the effect of demographic characteristics on each step in this process using a sample of US respondents. There are three main conclusions. First, at each stage there are significant differences between those on either sides of the divide. Starting with the digital divide, computer Internet use is uneven across various demographic groups, with younger, highly educated, affluent, and White adults more likely to use the Internet than others. The device divide was also apparent: mobile Internet use was unevenly distributed across demographics groups. In addition, the usage divide is reflected in the significant demographic differences between those who use mostly their phones to go online and those who use mostly their computers.

Second, I found that some demographic characteristics had different effects on the three transitions, which highlights the fact that each type of digital divide is unique. One rule of thumb for Internet use – that it decreases with age – still holds when considering all three levels of Internet use. Younger adults are more likely to make all three transitions; that is, from a non-user to a computer Internet user, then to a mobile Internet user, and then finally to becoming a mobile-mostly user. However, other rules of thumb – that Internet use increases with education or income – appear to be true for the first two transitions, but not when considering mobile-mostly use. In addition, the notion that non-Hispanic Black and Hispanic adults are less likely to use the Internet compared to White adults was only true for the first transition. It shifted when considering mobile Internet use and mobile-mostly Internet use; conditional on computer Internet use, non-Hispanic Black and Hispanic adults are actually more likely to make the transition to going online using their phones and Black adults were reliably more likely to become mobile-mostly users compared to White adults. Generally speaking, in the US the device divide looks a lot like the digital divide in terms of the demographics characteristics of people on either side, but the *usage* divide is quite unique. This is perhaps not surprising given the nature of the divides. While the first two divides have to do with adoption of a technology (computers and Internet-enabled phones), the third divide has to do with preferences toward a device that one is already using. Given the recent trends, the first two transitions seem almost inevitable for those who rely on technology while the third transition may not become widespread, given that most people prefer to use computers rather than their phones for complicated and long tasks (Robinson 2014). Of course this could change as phones evolve to feature larger screens (e.g., phablets) and more advanced computing capabilities.

Third, I found that one non-demographic variable – tablet use – was significantly associated with each of the transitions over and above demographic variables. This suggests that survey practitioners cannot correct all of the bias from omitting certain groups of Internet users by weighting on demographics characteristics. By contrast, the other variables – life quality and social trust – were not associated with the transitions over and above the demographics controls, suggesting that differences between those who are covered and not covered on these two particular survey variables can be accounted for by weighting on demographics characteristics. Perhaps variables related to technology are the ones that are more likely to be biased because they are likely to be correlated with Internet use. Future work should explore this for a larger set of survey variables of interest. In the meantime, to reduce potential coverage errors, online survey researchers would be wise to try to accommodate all online users if possible through use of a hybrid or adaptive design approach that optimizes their questionnaires for small devices.

It should be noted that this study used data from a telephone survey with a relatively low response rate, which may increase the risk of nonresponse bias. Nonetheless, this analysis did use weighting adjustments to help account for any potential nonresponse errors. That said, it would certainly be beneficial to conduct more research on this topic using a different survey mode (e.g., face-to-face) that could achieve higher response rates. That would also eliminate the possibility for differential measurement errors in the answers provided by landline and cell respondents. It should also be pointed out that the analysis uses cross-sectional data to observe aggregate level but not individual level change, the latter of which would be possible to observe if future researchers were to grapple with this same research topic using longitudinal data.

Moving forward, it is clear that the discussion about coverage bias in Web surveys will need to focus not only on the digital divide but also on the device divide and on the emerging divide between the growing number of individuals who prefer using their phone to go online and those who prefer to use their computer. This shift in Internet use is affecting errors of non-observation in Web surveys in new and complicated ways. The effects will continue to be influenced by the proportions of people in each Internet use group, the size of differences between users and non-users, and whether these differences can be accounted for by demographic variables.

Acknowledgements

I acknowledge the Pew Reseach Center for providing access to the data used in this analysis. They bear no responsibility for the interpretations or conclusions reached based on my analysis.

References

AAPOR. (2014). *Mobile Technologies for Conducting, Augmenting and Potentially Replacing Surveys: Report of the AAPOR Task Force on Emerging Technologies in Public Opinion Research*. Deerfield, IL: American Association for Public Opinion Research.

Antoun, C., & Couper, M. P. (2013, November). *Mobile-Mostly Internet Users and Selection Bias in Traditional Web Surveys*. Paper presented at the annual meeting of the Midwest Association for Public Opinion Research, Chicago, USA.

Bethlehem, J. (2010). Selection Bias in Web Surveys: Selection Bias in Web Surveys. *International Statistical Review*, 78(2), 161–188. DOI: http://dx.doi.org/10.1111/j.1751-5823.2010.00112.x

Blumberg, S. J., & Luke, J. V. (2013). *Wireless Substitution: Early Release of Estimates From the National Health Interview Survey, January–June 2013*. Center for Disease Control Report. Retrieved from http://www.cdc.gov/nchs/data/nhis/earlyrelease/wireless201312.pdf

Couper, M. P., Kapteyn, A., Schonlau, M., & Winter, J. (2007). Noncoverage and Nonresponse in an Internet Survey. *Social Science Research*, 36(1), 131–148. DOI: http://dx.doi.org/10.1016/j.ssresearch.2005.10.002

Curtin, R., Presser, S., & Singer, E. (2005). Changes in telephone survey nonresponse over the past quarter century. *Public opinion quarterly*, 69(1), 87-98.

de Bruijne, M., & Wijnant, A. (2014). Mobile Response in Web Panels. *Social Science Computer Review*, 32(6), 728–742. DOI: http://dx.doi.org/10.1177/0894439314525918

Dever, J. A., Rafferty, A., & Valliant, R. (2008). Internet Surveys: Can Statistical Adjustments Eliminate Coverage Bias. *Survey Research Methods*, 2, 47–62.

Duggan, M., & Rainie, L. (2012). *Cell Phone Activities 2012*. Pew Research Center's Internet & American Life Project.

Duggan, M., & Smith, A. (2013). *Cell Internet Use 2013*. Pew Research Center's Internet & American Life Project.

Fuchs, M., & Busse, B. (2009). The Coverage Bias of Mobile Web Surveys across European Countries. *International Journal of Internet Science*, 4(1), 21–33.

Groves, R. M., & Peytcheva, E. (2008). The impact of nonresponse rates on nonresponse bias a meta-analysis. *Public opinion quarterly*, 72(2), 167–189. DOI: http://dx.doi.org/10.1093/poq/nfn011

Lenhart, A. (2003). *The Ever-Shifting Internet Population: A New Look at Internet Access and the Digital Divide*. Washington, DC: The Pew Internet and American Life Project.

Lipsman, A., & Aquino, C. (2013). *Mobile Future in Focus*. comScore Report. Retrieved from http://www.comscore.com/Insights/Presentations-and-Whitepapers/2013/2013-Mobile-Future-in-Focus

Metzler, A., & Fuchs, M. (2014, December). *Coverage Error in Mobile Web Surveys Across European Countries*. Paper presented at the Internet Survey Methodology Workshop, Bozen-Bolzano, Italy.

Mohorko, A., de Leeuw, E., & Hox, J. (2013). Internet Coverage and Coverage Bias in Europe: Developments Across Countries and Over Time. *Journal of Official Statistics*, *29*(4), 609–622. DOI: http://dx.doi.org/10.2478/jos-2013-0042

NTIA (National Telecommunications and Information Administration). (1995, July). *Falling Through the Net: A Survey of the »Have Nots« in Rural and Urban America*.

Pearce, K. E., & Rice, R. E. (2013). Digital Divides From Access to Activities: Comparing Mobile and Personal Computer Internet Users. *Journal of Communication*, *63*(4), 721–744. DOI: http://dx.doi.org/10.1111/jcom.12045

Peterson, G. (2012, May). *Unintended Mobile Respondents*. Paper presented at the CASRO Technology Conference, New York, USA.

Pew Center for the People and the Press. (1995). *Technology in the American household; Americans going online... Explosive growth, uncertain destinations*. Retrieved from http://www.people-press.org/1995/10/16/americans-going-online-explosive-growth-uncertain-destinations/

Pew Research Center. (2012). *Spring 2012 tracking survey* [Questionnaire and Topline report]. Retrieved from http://www.pewinternet.org/files/old-media/Files/Questionnaire/2012/PIP_Just_In_Time_topline.pdf

Poushter, J., Bell, J., & Oates, R. (2015). Internet Seen as Positive Influence on Education but Negative on Morality in Emerging and Developing Nations. *Pew Research Center*.

Revilla, M., Toninelli, D., Ochoa, C., & Loewe, G. (2014). *Do Online Access Panels Really Need to Allow and Adapt Surveys to Mobile Devices?* Barcelona: Universitat Pompeu Fabra, RECSM Working Paper Number 41. Retrieved from http://www.upf.edu/survey/_pdf/RECSM_wp041.pdf

Robinson, O. (2014). Finding Simplicity in a Multi-Device World. *GfK online article*. Retrieved from http://blog.gfk.com/2014/03/finding-simplicity-in-a-multi-device-world

Smith, A. (2012). Nearly Half of American Adults Are Smartphone Owners. *Pew Research Center*.

Tourangeau, R., Conrad, F., & Couper, M. (2013). *The Science of Web Surveys*. Oxford: Oxford University Press. DOI: http://dx.doi.org/10.1093/acprof:oso/9780199747047.001.0001

Townsend, L., & Rios, H. (2011)..*Defragmenting Mobile Research - How to Successfully Combine the Wide Array of Available Mobile Tools and Create a Highly Effective Mobile Platform*. Kinesis Survey Software White Paper. Retrieved from http://www.kinesissurvey.com/files/DefragmentingMobileResearch_KinesisWhitepaper.pdf

Zickuhr, K. (2013). Who's not online and why. *Pew Research Center*.

CHAPTER 8

Who Has Access to Mobile Devices in an Online Opt-in Panel? An Analysis of Potential Respondents for Mobile Surveys

Melanie Revilla*, Daniele Toninelli†, Carlos Ochoa‡ and German Loewe‡

*RECSM - Universitat Pompeu Fabra, Spain, melanie.revilla@upf.edu,
†University of Bergamo, Italy, daniele.toninelli@unibg.it,
‡Netquest, Spain

Abstract

In most countries the spread of mobile devices in the general population has increased very quickly in the last years, changing people's habits of accessing and using the web. Because of this, if one wants to involve respondents who access the web with the new devices, it is necessary to adapt web surveys to these devices. Nowadays, even if some probability-based online panels exist, the large majority of web surveys are done by means of non-probability-based panels (also called 'opt-in' or 'access' panels). People volunteer to participate in these panels. Thus, we can expect that the spread of mobile devices in these panels differs from the spread of mobile devices in the general population and is probably higher. However, little is known about the exact spread of different mobile devices (tablets and smartphones) within the population of panelists in access panels. Moreover, little knowledge has been acquired about which combination of devices panelists have, in general and in different countries. However, this is crucial information, since access panels represent the majority of web surveys and the participation of the panelists in these surveys is conditioned by the equipment they own. Therefore, in this chapter we study data

How to cite this book chapter:
Revilla, M, Toninelli, D, Ochoa, C and Loewe, G. 2015. Who Has Access to Mobile
    Devices in an Online Opt-in Panel? An Analysis of Potential Respondents for Mobile
    Surveys. In: Toninelli, D, Pinter, R & de Pedraza, P (eds.) *Mobile Research Methods:
    Opportunities and Challenges of Mobile Research Methodologies*, Pp. 119–139. London:
    Ubiquity Press. DOI: http://dx.doi.org/10.5334/bar.h. License: CC-BY 4.0.

from the Netquest online panel to get a more precise idea of the proportion of potential respondents in access online panels who would participate to surveys through mobile devices. The aim is mainly to evaluate the current spread of devices and their combination in a set of countries not studied before: Spain, Portugal and Latin American countries.

Keywords

Opt-in web panel, web surveys, mobile device ownership, mobile device access, Netquest

Introduction

It is clear that the spread of mobile devices (in particular smartphones and tablets) in the general population has increased very quickly in the last years, changing people's habits of accessing and using the web. A simultaneous quick increase of the active mobile Internet usage was observed. Worldwide, the mobile Internet penetration grew from 7% in 2008 to 23% in 2012 and 29% in 2013 (Statista 2014). According to the Statista (2014) study, the mobile Internet penetration is expected to overtake the fixed-broadband penetration in 2017 (reaching 54% and 51%, respectively). In some countries, this overtaking is already happening: for example, in terms of usage, according to StatCounter Global Stats (August 2014),[26] the mobile has overtaken the fixed-broadband Internet usage in India (70.4% vs 28.2%), South Africa (55.7% vs 38.7%) and Saudi Arabia (51.2% vs 40.5%). In 2013, the mobile usage represented 25% of the overall web usage, according to Smart Insights (2014) and KPCB (2014). This corresponds to an increase of 14% in comparison to the previous year. In particular, according to KPCB (2014), in Europe the mobile access is 16% of all web usage (+8% in comparison to the previous year), and in North America it represents 19% of all web usage (+11% in one year). StatCounter Global Stats (2014) confirms these findings: the percentage of desktop Internet traffic was 63.6% in October 2014 (−32 percentage points compared to January 2011), whereas for mobile usage the percentage has grown rapidly from the 4.3% registered on January 2011 to 29.8% in October 2014 (+25.5 percentage points). In this same month of October 2014, tablets accounted for 6.53% of global Internet usage, whereas this percentage, just 12 months before, was 4.54%. Thus, an increase of 1.99 percentage points was observed for tablet-based Internet use.

---

[26] StatCounter is a web analytics service that tracks over three million web sites worldwide. Every month, billions of page views of these tracked web sites are analyzed, recording characteristics of the web usage such as use of browser or of mobile devices. For further information, see: http://gs.statcounter.com/faq.

Several factors contributed to this spreading process: for instance, the generally decreasing costs of mobile web connection or the improved quality of networks. But this trend is expected to be further encouraged by the wider distribution of mobile devices characterizing most countries. This process of a wide spread of mobile devices in web usage, according to recently observed data, will probably continue in the near future. Because of this, many researchers started thinking that web surveys needed to be adapted to these new devices. For instance, de Bruijne and Wijnant (2013: 483) claim that if the use of mobile devices is already considered a 'serious new alternative [...] for web-based self-administered surveys', probably, with more developed technologies for both smartphones and tablets, in the close future it will become 'not only an alternative way to reach respondents, but perhaps even an indispensable one'.

Nowadays, even if some probability-based online panels exist (e.g. the Knowledge panel in the USA, the LISS panel in the Netherlands, the ELIPSS panel in France or the German Internet Panel), the large majority of web surveys are done by non-probability-based panels, also called 'opt-in' or 'access' panels. Because people volunteer to participate in these panels, we can expect that the spread of devices in these panels differs from the spread of devices in the general population and is probably higher. However, little is known about the exact spread of different mobile devices (tablets and smartphones) for people registered in access panels across time and in different countries. Also, little is known about which combination of devices panelists in access panels have at their disposal: how many of them have only a PC, only a mobile device (and which one) or a combination of both a PC and one or several mobile devices?

This is crucial information, since this kind of panels represents the majority of web surveys and since the participation of the panelists in these surveys is conditioned by the equipment they own. Indeed, access panels institutes/companies normally do not provide panelists who do not have a piece of equipment with that piece of equipment so that they can still participate in the surveys, contrarily to what probability-based panels usually do. Therefore, to get an idea of the proportion of potential mobile respondents in access online panels, information is needed about the current spread of such devices within panelists in these panels.

In this chapter, we will use the Netquest online panel data to evaluate the current spread of devices and their combination in a set of countries not studied before: Spain, Portugal and five Latin American countries (Argentina, Brazil, Chile, Colombia and Mexico). The next section will summarize what is already known about this topic, focusing on the state of the art of the current Internet coverage around the world and, more specifically, on the mobile web access penetration. In the following section, we will provide new evidence about the spread of mobile devices in the Netquest panel, studying both the proportion of panelists who own or have regular access to PC and mobile devices (smartphones and tablets) and the combinations of devices the panelists have. Then we will study whether there are significant differences between the groups of panelists who have only a PC and the ones who own at least one mobile device or own no devices at all and between the panelists who own only mobile devices and the others. Finally, the last section will summarize and discuss the main results, together with the limitations of this work and with some ideas to further develop this research.

Internet coverage and mobile web access

The Internet coverage is evolving very quickly. According to the latest data available (updated on December 31, 2013), the worldwide penetration of Internet, considering an estimated population of 7.18 billion people, is 39.0% (source: Internet World Stats 2014). The same percentage, updated on June 30, 2012, was 34.3%. This means that the coverage of the worldwide population has increased by 4.7 percentage points in just one year and a half. If we consider a longer time range, the Internet penetration for the worldwide population increased by 676.3% from 2000 to 2014 (the increase percentage between 2000 and 2012 was 566.4). Nevertheless, this general trend varies a lot by world region. In fact, the Internet coverage percentage ranges from the 21.3% registered in Africa to the 31.7% observed in Asia, up to the 68.6% in European countries and to the 84.9% in North America. The growth rates from 2000 to 2014 are also very different, ranging from the 177.8% observed in North America to the 5219.3% registered in Africa. If we take a more detailed look, even within the same region, the observed penetration rates of Internet varies a lot: for example, in Europe the minimum penetration observed is 41.8%, registered for Ukraine, and the highest one is 96.5%, for Iceland. In **Figure 1**, the Internet penetration rate by country is represented.

Nevertheless, one can ask the following question: if the Internet coverage increased so quickly in the last few years, what about the mobile access to the web? A lot of studies show that the mobile web penetration increased a lot in the last years too. According to a Eurobarometer study (Fuchs &Busse 2009), 31% of the European population had access to a mobile Internet device in 2007, which is 5 percentage points higher than in 2005. Nielsen Mobile (2008) also highlights the growing importance of the mobile access phenomenon. In the first quarter of 2008, there were 254 million of mobile subscribers in the US; this subscription number generated US$1.7 billion in revenue, an amount that had quickly increased if compared to the US$5 billion in total revenue observed in the entire year of 2007.

Coming to closer times, in December 2011, 35% of EU citizens owning a personal mobile phone had access to the Internet through their mobile phones (Eurobarometer 2012). According to other research developed by Statistics Netherlands (2012), the mobile access rates continued to grow very quickly thereafter. In the Netherlands, 96% of the 12–75 years old used Internet in 2012, and from 2007 to 2012 the percentage of these users who accessed the

Figure 1: Internet penetration by countries (% of population).

Note: red = no statistics available.
Source: http://commons.wikimedia.org/wiki/File:Internet_Penetration.png; updated on Jan. 2012.

Internet by mobile devices has tripled: 60% of Internet users accessed the web by means of mobile devices in the three months before they carried out the survey. In comparison to the previous year, a growth of 10 percentage points was observed. The growth is particularly high for young people: in 2007, 21% of the 12–25 years old regularly used mobile devices to go online, whereas in 2012, the same category increased to 86% (27% of the 12–75 years old people accessed Internet via mobile phones, 11% via tablets). Focusing on the different devices, in 2012 the preferred ones were mobile phones (small and handy, used by 47% of mobile Internet users, 66% of them daily), but tablets (19%) were also regularly used (Statistics Netherlands 2012). Nevertheless, there is still a non-negligible percentage of Internet users (e.g. 40% in the Netherlands) who do not use mobile devices to access the web. This is mainly because they do not need to connect themselves to the Internet if they are outside home or outside their workplace, or due to the connection's costs. Regarding this last aspect, it was highlighted in a Eurobarometer (2012) study that about 43% of mobile Internet users limit their mobile Internet use due to concerns about charges. The most concerned about mobile Internet charges are Belgian (62%), Irish (60%) and Greek (60%) people, whereas lower percentages of concern are registered in the Netherlands (29%), Sweden (29%) or Luxembourg (28%).

Further data about the spread of mobile web show that between January 2012 and September 2013, access to the web by mobile web browser increased from 8.49% to 17.81% worldwide (StatCounter Global Stats 2013). de Bruijne and Wijnant (2013) studied what kind of connection was used to access Internet by analysing the CentERPanel data collected in the Netherlands: 28.7% of the panel members involved (14 years and older) accessed to web via smartphones, and 19.1% via tablets. This is consistent with the KPCB (2014) statement that 30% of all mobile users are smartphone users. More recently, StatCounter Global Stats (2014) observed that the worldwide use of mobile devices to surf the Internet has increased by 67% from September 2013 to the same month of 2014. If we consider the global mobile data traffic, the growth registered in 2013 is of 81% (Cisco VNI Mobile 2014). Cisco VNI Mobile (2014) also forecasted that the global mobile data traffic will grow nearly 11-fold between 2013 and 2018. This corresponds to a compound annual growth rate of 61%.

If these are the general figures, the situation changes a lot when considering different countries or regions. Analysing the mobile web penetration in earlier years, Fuchs and Busse (2009) noticed that the rates were very different from country to country: in 2007 in Europe, rates were varying from 18% in Romania and Bulgaria to 49% in Luxembourg. The same authors noticed that no clear pattern was observed for mobile web access rate: the coverage was mostly driven by various activities of network service providers in different markets. If we consider more recent data, according to a Eurobarometer (2012) study which referred to December 2011 in comparison to the first part of that year (March–April 2011), a marginal increase of the proportion of

	October 2012		October 2014		Desktop change (% points; 2014 vs 2012)	Mobile change (% points; 2014 vs 2012)
	Desktop	Mobile	Desktop	Mobile		
Argentina	95.6	4.5	79.9	20.1	−16.3	+15,6
Brazil	94.5	5.5	74.7	25.3	−20.9	+19.8
Chile	94.6	5.4	60.9	39.1	−35.7	+33.7
Colombia	96.8	3.2	79.3	20.7	−18.1	+17.5
Mexico	91.7	8.3	64.0	36.0	−30.2	+27.7
Portugal	96.2	3.8	78.3	21.7	−18.6	+17.9
Spain	90.1	9.9	56.6	43.4	−37.1	+33.5

Table 1: Desktop and mobile web usage by country (2012 and 2014).

respondents who own a mobile phone subscription allowing them to access the Internet was observed between both periods (+1%). But, again, this general figure varies a lot if one compares different countries: for the UK, Slovenia, Finland and Malta, for example, a growth of 6% was observed, similar to the level registered in Luxembourg (+5%); on the other hand, a fall in mobile Internet access was observed in Portugal (−12%) and in the Czech Republic (−7%). According to the same study, the percentage of EU citizens owning a personal mobile phone who had access to the Internet through such a kind of device is highest in Sweden (63%), the UK (58%) and Slovenia (57%), whereas this situation is still less common in Bulgaria (13%), Portugal (16%), Italy (17%) and Romania (18%).

Table 1 helps in focusing the analysis of the current web usage (and of its spread in the last few years) specifically on the countries that will be studied in this chapter: Argentina, Brazil, Chile, Colombia, Mexico, Portugal and Spain. In particular, the table shows the percentages of desktop and mobile web usage,[27] comparing October 2014 with October 2012 (data source: StatCounter Global Stats 2014).

The Internet traffic by device has changed a lot even in the last two years only. If in October 2012, the desktop accesses covered more than 90% of web traffic in the seven considered countries (with a peak of more than 96% in Colombia and Portugal), after 24 months the same percentage dropped by more than 15 percentage points. But these general figures are only the reflection of the different levels of changes observed in different countries. The drop is indeed mostly relevant in Chile (from 94.6% to 60.9%), in Mexico (from 91.7% to 64.0%) and in Spain (from 90.1% to 56.6%), whereas it is observed at a lower

---

[27] StatCounter tracks tablets as a separate category. Nevertheless, in **Table 1** the 'Mobile devices' data also include tablets: we merged the two categories for the sake of clarity.

level for example in Argentina (from 95.6% to 79.9%), in Portugal (from 96.2% to 78.3%) or Colombia (from 96.8% to 79.3%).

One of the possible consequences of this is the considerable increase in terms of mobile usage of the web observed for Chile (from 5.4% to 39.1%, corresponding to +33.7 percentage points), Spain (from 9.9% to 43.4%; +33.5 p.p.) and Mexico (from 8.3% to 36.0%; +27.7 p.p.). In 2014, the spread of mobile traffic shows lower levels (between 20% and 26%) for Brazil (25.3%; +19.8 p.p.) Portugal (21.7%; +17.9 p.p.), Colombia (20.7%; +17.5 p.p.) and Argentina (20.1%; +15.6 p.p.).

To sum up, a lot of research has been made showing that overall a fast increase is observed in most countries in Internet coverage and mobile access to the web. Nevertheless, the necessity of further research is emphasized by the following factors: first, the noticeable differences in mobile Internet coverage/ usage penetration rate and in its patterns over time from country to country (e.g. Eurobarometer 2012; Fuchs & Busse 2009; StatCounter Global Stats 2014); second, the potential different purposes and factors that push people to the mobile usage[28]; and third, most previous results refer to the general population, but we can expect differences for mobile spread between the general population and the participants of access online panels.

Some agencies or services, such as StatCounter, already provide detailed and updated data concerning web usage (see **Table 1**), but this information does not really fit the purposes of our research for two main reasons. First, StatCounter data are focused on web traffic; thus, for instance, the same mobile users can be counted several times as they access several web pages with the same device. Second, our study is mainly focused on panelists and their coverage by mobile access, not on the general population.

Online panel suveys need to know specifically what the spread of mobile devices within panel members is and who the persons susceptible to answer (or not answer) to the surveys through mobile devices are. We assume that the spread of mobile devices will be even larger in this specific population of web panelists, but how much larger? And are there groups of panelists with different levels of mobile coverage? Moreover, the urgency to develop a more detailed research increases with the fact that mobile devices are not only replacing more traditional devices like PCs (desktop or laptops), but are also complementing them in many cases, such that more and more individuals own not only one device but a combination of devices. For example, it was highlighted that 'mobile Internet is used as a complimentary mean for accessing the web; respondents who have mobile Internet have Internet in their homes as well' (Eurobarometer 2012: 9). Thus, it also becomes relevant to understand which combinations of devices the panelists have regular access to. Very little

---

[28] For example, in Japan the mobile web is very well spread because it is the main way to watch television and access Internet, whereas mobile web access is less important in other countries where there are already landline infrastructures for both TV and Internet (Okazaki 2007).

is known about this topic, in particular in some geographical areas like Latin America. That is why, in the following parts of this chapter, we will focus on the spread of mobile devices for participants to an access online panel in seven countries that have not been studied much before from this perspective.

New evidence from the Netquest panel

Netquest (www.netquest.com) is an online fieldwork company founded in 2001 that started its first online panel in 2006, in Spain. Currently, it is also present in Portugal and Latin America, with more than 450,000 panelists truly active[29] and 4 millions of completed surveys every year. What differentiates Netquest from other online access panels is that it is the only one in the Latin American and South European region accredited with the ISO 26362 quality standard. Netquest recruits people corresponding to the profile it needs to participate in the panel. The potential respondents are selected from different databases of users of many websites who agreed to receive emails. Once they have joined the panel, for each completed survey, panelists get points that they can exchange for gifts. While most of the surveys sent by Netquest were developed for computers (desktops and laptops), the company noticed an increasing demand from both some clients and some panelists to use mobile devices to design or answer the surveys (with direct requests or comments and with numbers of attempts to complete the surveys through mobile devices). In order to get more information on this phenomenon, Netquest provided the necessary data to study in a more in-depth manner the spread of mobile participation within its panelists to determine which strategy to adopt for the years to come. The results of the analyses are presented in the next subsections. By using these data, we get new evidence about the spread of mobile access in Central and Latin America, and in Portugal and Spain, and for a very large number of panelists.

Owning different devices

Netquest has a system of continuous profiling of its panelists by means of different modules. Each module deals with a different topic. When respondents are filtered out of a survey, they get one of these profiling modules. Using this system, Netquest accumulates information about as many panelists as possible in order to be able to target specific populations and/or to model different behaviors or attitudes. The order in which respondents get the modules depends on the level of priority Netquest attributes to the corresponding topic. Starting

---

[29] We define as 'truly active' a member who participated to at least one survey sent by Netquest in the last 12 months. Data updated in November 2014.

from the end of 2012, Netquest introduced two modules: one about the equipment of the respondents, in which they are asked, among other things, if they
have a desktop PC, a laptop and/or a tablet; and one about new technologies, in
which one of the questions asks if they own a smartphone.

Figure 2 shows the percentages over time of panelists who own the different
devices by country.[30] The data are aggregated by quarter. The first data correspond to the first quarter of 2013 (except for Spain, where the modules started
later). Even if some of the information was available for the end of 2012, it is
not shown in the graphs, because it was incomplete. It should be clear that the
information at different points in time is based on different panelists. Thus, the
number of respondents to these modules varies from month to month and from
country to country (cf. Appendix 1). Nevertheless, overall these results represent a huge amount of panelists for which this information is known: more than
190,000 for the first module, and more than 250,000 for the second one.

The first chart of Figure 2 shows the average of all countries. It highlights
that the proportion of panelists who own a smartphone (79.9%) is as high as
the one of those who have a laptop (80.7%) in the first quarter of 2013. Both are
about 10 percentage points higher than the proportion of panelists who own a
desktop PC (71.9%). Moreover, the proportion of smartphone owners seems to
have slowly overtaken the percentage of laptop owners (see the data for the last
quarter in the same chart: 82.0% for smartphones vs 76.6% for laptops). Generally, the proportion of panelists with a tablet is much lower (around 30–40%),
but it is also increasing over time, even very quickly in some countries (e.g.
in Chile, where the percentage is more than doubled in just one year). On the
contrary, the proportion of panelists owning a desktop PC tends to decrease: on
average, it loses about five percentage points in one year, and this trend is confirmed in all the single countries. Even if there are differences across countries
in the observed percentages of smartphone and tablet owners, clearly a large
majority of panelists owns mobile devices, and we can reasonably expect that
this phenomenon will continue to spread further in the future (at least on the
tablet side). On the other hand, Figure 2 already suggests that probably fewer
and fewer panelists will own a computer (at least a desktop one); these findings
seem to confirm the forecasts of some studies that are expecting the mobile web
penetration to overtake the fixed broadband penetration in the next few years
(Statista 2014), as seen in section 1.

Combination of devices

Figure 2 only provides information about owning different devices, without
allowing to discriminate if respondents own only one device or a combination

---

[30]   The questions asked are: 'Do you have a desktop PC?', 'Do you have a laptop?', 'Do you have a
tablet?', and 'Do you have a smartphone?'.

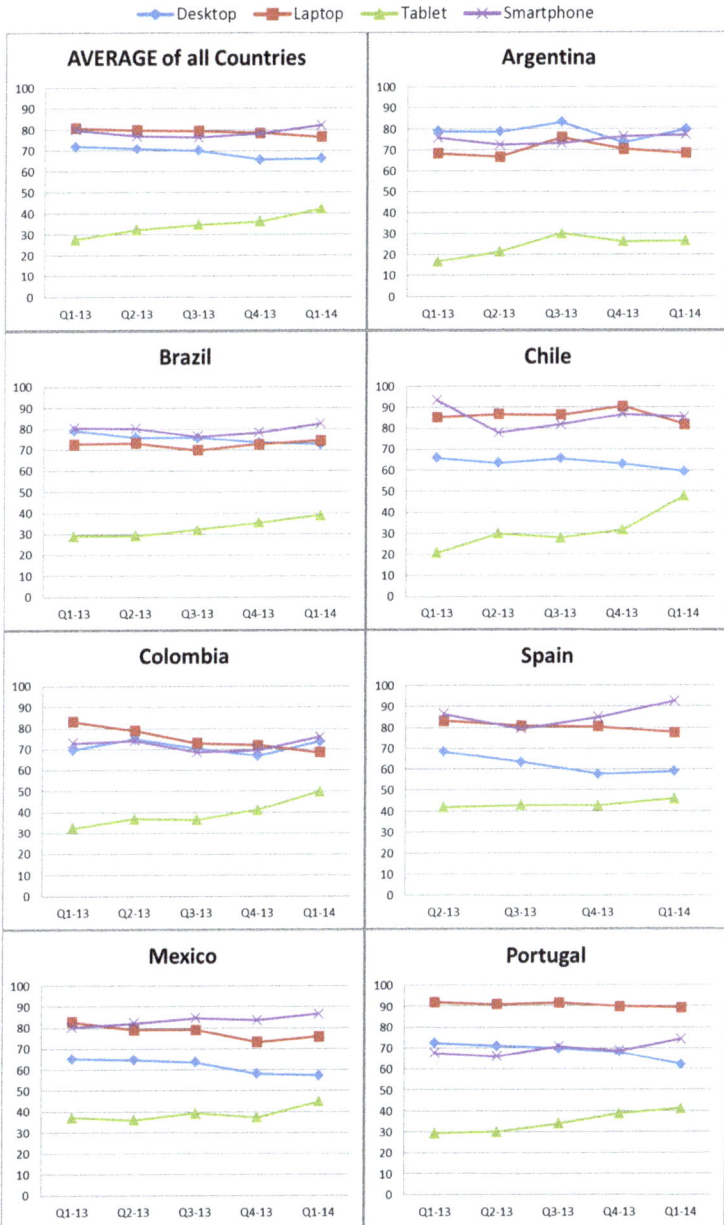

Figure 2: Percentages of panelists who own different devices.

*Note: Q1-13 means the first quarter year of 2013, Q2-13 means the second quarter year of 2013, etc.;
Average = non-weighted average of the values of the different countries.*

of two or more devices. To get this more detailed information, we need to cross the data from the two modules previously mentioned. In doing so, we are reducing the number of observations at each point in time quite a lot. For this reason, instead of looking at each quarter year, we have aggregated the data of the different quarters, starting with the second quarter year of 2013 because there are not enough data before. **Figure 3** presents the percentages of panelists who answered both modules and who have only one device or a combination of two or three (the two kinds of PC, fixed and laptop, are shown combined for the sake of clarity).

Again, **Figure 3** shows that, even if there are some variations in the size of the proportions across countries, overall, the same main trends are observed. In all countries, the largest percentage corresponds to the combination of a computer and a smartphone (42.3% on average). The following largest category is the combination of the three devices (computer + tablet + smartphone, 28.9% on average). On average only 20.3% of panelists own only one kind of device. Therefore, the majority of potential respondents can really choose to answer surveys through one or another device. However, there is still a non-negligible part of panelists who have only a computer (from 12.9% in Chile to 24.1% in Portugal; 17.7% on average). Almost no panelists have only a tablet (0.2%) and very few of them have only a smartphone (2.4% on average, with a maximum level observed for Mexico: 3.5%) or have no devices and for instance go to an Internet café or complete the survey at work (on average 1.6%; this percentage rises to 2.2% for Mexico and to 2.3% for Colombia).

Looking at the evolution over time of owning these devices, **Figure 4** shows the differences (in percentage points) between the proportions of panelists with one, two or three devices, comparing the last available point in time (Q1 of 2014) and the first one (Q2 of 2013).

Figure 4 shows that the ownership of different devices has evolved quite a lot in about one year: for example, the proportion of panelists with three devices increased considerably (7.7 percentage points on average, with a peak of 14.7 percentage points for Colombia), while on the other hand the proportion of PC-only owners mainly decreased in all countries (by 7.8 percentage point on average, with a maximum of 11.9 percentage points lost for Colombia).

Additional access to different devices

So far, we focused the analysis on whether or not panelists owned different types of devices. However, we should note that panelists can also have access to some devices even if they do not own them: for instance, they can have regular access to a computer at their workplace or at a library. In order to take this important aspect into account, we studied data from a survey completed by around 1,000 Netquest respondents within each country (quotas were set by age and gender to obtain, in each country, a sample representative of the complete panel

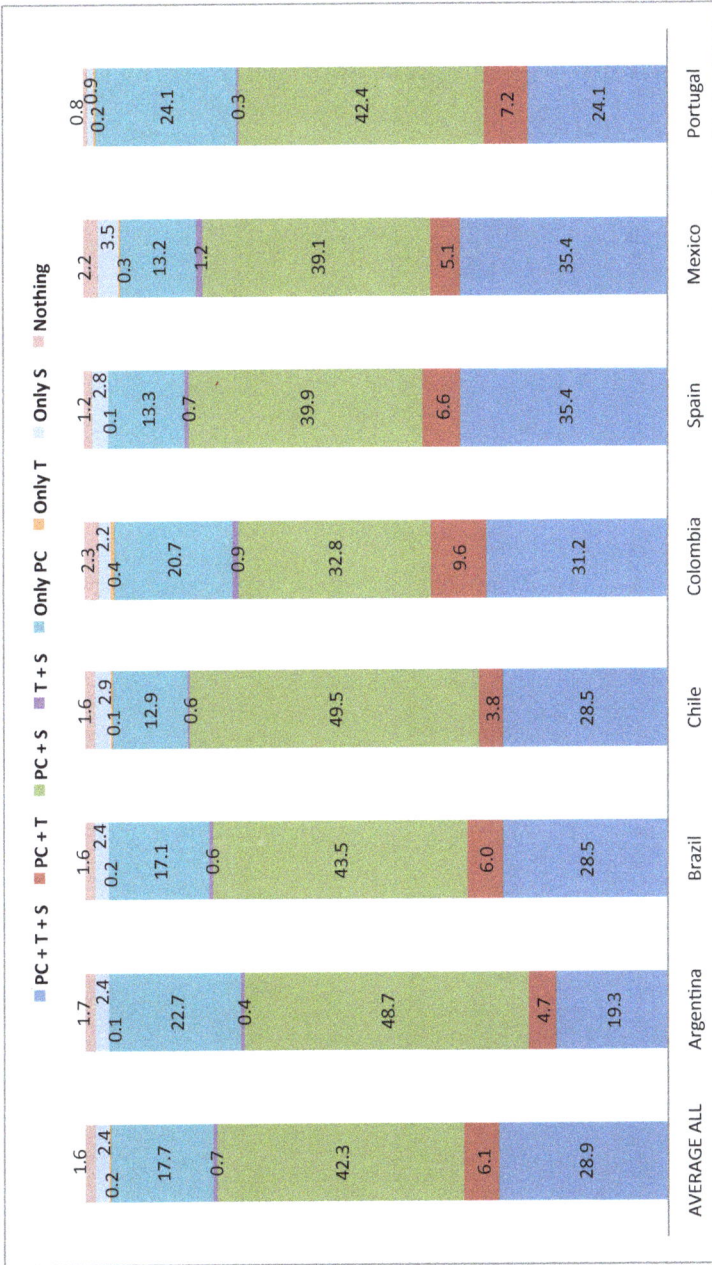

Figure 3: Percentages of panelists who own different combinations of devices.

Note: T = tablet; S = smartphone; PC = desktop + laptop. AverageAll = non-weighted average of the values of the different countries.

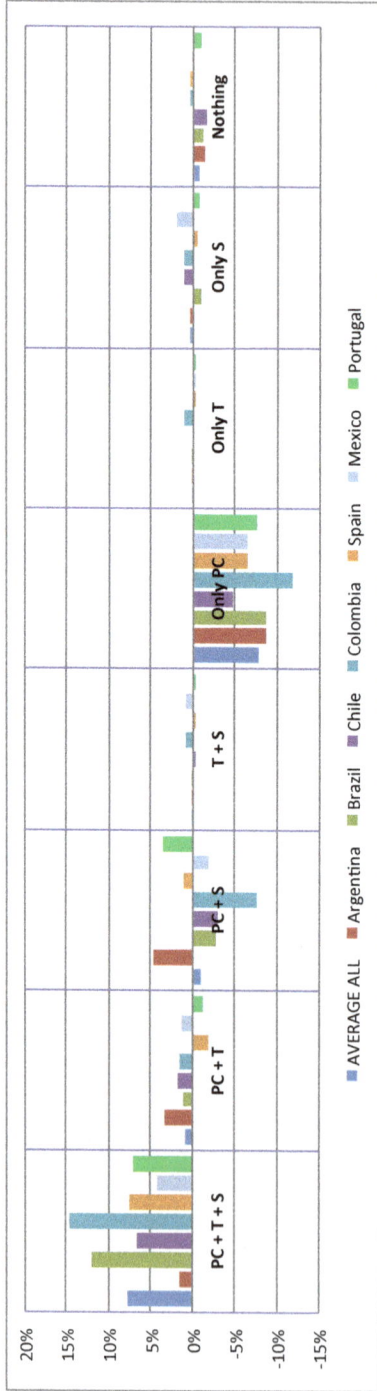

Figure 4: Differences in combination of devices between Q1 of 2014 and Q2 of 2013 (percentage points).

Note. AverageAll = non-weighted average of the values of the different countries.

population). Respondents were asked if they owned different devices, and, in the case where they answered 'no', they were asked if they had a regular access to these devices. In **Table 2** the additional percentages of respondents who have regular access to the devices, even though they do not own them, are shown.

Table 2 shows that there is an additional percentage of respondents, between 10.5% (observed in Spain) and 19.7% (in Chile), who have regular access to a desktop PC, even though they do not own one; the unweighted average over countries is 14.3%. Regarding laptops, 8.9% of respondents (unweighted general average) have access to one, in spite of not owning one: the lowest percentage is observed for Spain (4.9%), and the highest one for Colombia (12.9%). The highest percentage of access to a device without owning it is registered for tablets (16.3%, general unweighted average; ranging from 10.8% in Portugal to 22.2% in Colombia); the additional usage for smartphones is only 5.7% (from 2.1% for Spain to 9.2% for Colombia).

From these results, we can presume that at least part of the considered panelists could be susceptible to answer surveys using devices that they do not own but regularly have access to. However, it can also happen that they have access to these devices in places or at times which will not allow or encourage them to participate in surveys. Therefore, it is difficult to estimate the real exact spread of the availability of different devices among panelists. This would need to be further studied.

In any case, we can conclude that overall, by not allowing respondents to answer the surveys through mobile devices, one would really exclude very few panelists for coverage issue, since very few do not have a computer (fixed or laptop), and even fewer do not have at least a regular access to a computer. Nevertheless, the panelists may decide to take part or not in a survey depending on the possibility to answer by means of different devices (including tablets and

	Fixed PC	Laptop	Tablet	Smartphone
Argentina	11.8	11.6	17.6	8.8
Brazil	15.2	10.8	12.6	4.9
Chile	19.7	6.8	19.6	4.3
Colombia	11.7	12.9	22.2	9.2
Spain	10.5	4.9	12.0	2.1
Mexico	13.3	9.2	19.3	5.1
Portugal	17.9	6.2	10.8	5.6
Average All	**14.3**	**8.9**	**16.3**	**5.7**

Table 2: Additional percentages of respondents who have regular access to the devices.

Note: Average All = non-weighted average of the values of the different countries.

smartphones) and according to their preferences for these devices, since most panelists have the choice between at least two devices (and about 25–35% of them even between three devices). Further research is needed in this direction. Besides, even if it is a small group that would be excluded, this group could be very different from the rest of the panelists; thus the impact on the representativeness of the panel may be problematic. Therefore, in the next section we compare the characteristics of panelists who own different devices.

Differences across groups: logistic regression analysis

In this section, by means of two logistic regressions, we aim at understanding to what extent there are differences in the characteristics of groups of panelists who differ in terms of ownership of devices. In particular, we focus on the following main available variables: gender (dummy variable: 1 = men), age (in categories), education (from lower to higher diploma; categories vary for different countries) and number of household members (numeric). In order to see which variables really affect the ownership of different devices, we first study the effect of the explanatory variables mentioned above on the fact that respondents own only a PC rather than at least one mobile device or no device at all. **Table 3** presents the coefficients of this first logit.

According to the results shown in **Table 3**, in all countries there is a significant effect of age (higher probability to have only a PC for older respondents) and of education (lower probability to have only a PC for more highly educated respondents). Gender has a significant effect in Colombia, Spain, Mexico and Portugal, but not in Argentina, Brazil and Chile. Generally, whether it is significant or not, the gender's effect is negative, meaning that men are less likely to

Own only a PC	Argentina	Brazil	Chile	Colombia	Spain	Mexico	Portugal
Men	−0.24	−0.12	−0.27	−0.31*	−0.64**	−0.51**	−0.43**
Age	0.35**	0.32**	0.56**	0.26**	0.44**	0.33**	0.42**
Education	−0.35**	−0.50**	−0.33**	−0.50**	−0.41**	−0.19**	−0.41**
No. household	0.07	0.13**	−0.05	0.05	−0.20*	0.08	−0.01
Constant	−0.94	−0.69	−1.75**	0.18	−1.08	−0.99	−0.73
PseudoR^2	0.0499	0.0527	0.0765	0.0459	0.0940	0.0592	0.0602
No. obs.	N = 1000	N = 1011	N = 1000	N = 1001	N = 1002	N = 1005	N = 1000

Table 3: Logit of respondents who own only a PC versus the others.

Note: ** $p < 0.05$; * $p < 0.10$; No. household = number of persons in the household; No. obs = number of observations.

Own only a mobile device	Argentina	Brazil	Chile	Colombia	Spain	Mexico	Portugal
Men	0.06	−0.50	0.31	−1.44	−0.32	−0.67	−0.52
Age	−0.14	−0.15	−0.17	−0.17	−0.05	−0.34	0.01
Education	−1.34**	−0.39	−0.50**	−0.32	−0.64*	−0.38**	−0.61*
No. household	0.25**	−0.11	−0.46*	0.06	−0.29	0.06	0.26**
Constant	−0.71	−1.25	0.10	−2.55	−0.44	0.06	−2.26
No. Obs.	N = 1000	N = 1011	N = 1000	N = 1001	N = 1002	N = 1005	N = 1000

Table 4: ReLogit of respondents who own only mobile devices versus the others.

*Note: ** $p < 0.05$; * $p \leq 0.10$; No. household = number of persons in the household; No. obs = number of observations.*

own only a PC. The number of persons in the household has a significant effect only in two countries: Brazil (positive effect) and Spain (negative effect). Thus, overall, panelists who own only a PC differ from panelists with at least one kind of mobile device or no device at all in terms of age and education, and, in the majority of the countries, also in terms of gender.

Second, we study the respondents who own only mobile devices (smartphones, tablets or a combination of both) versus the others. Because the proportions of respondents who own only mobile devices are very small in each country, a classic logistic regression may lead to biased estimates. Instead, we use the RELOGIT command in Stata (Tomz, King & Zeng 1999).[31] The results of the analyses are shown in **Table 4**.

Table 4 shows that age and gender do not have any significant effect in any of the countries analyzed. On the contrary, education has a significant negative effect in Argentina, Chile and Mexico ($p < 0.05$) and an effect on the edge of significance in Spain and Portugal ($p = 0.10$). This means that in most countries, less educated respondents are more likely to have only mobile devices. Thus, allowing panelists to answer through mobiles devices and adapting surveys to facilitate their completion on mobile devices may favour the participation of less educated people, who have a higher probability of owning only mobile devices. Finally, the number of persons in the household has a significant positive effect in Argentina and Portugal and a significant negative effect in Chile. On the one hand, the positive effect may be linked to the fact that the

---

31 As defined by its authors, 'RELOGIT is a suite of programs for estimating and interpreting logit results when the sample is unbalanced (one outcome is rarer than the other) [...] RELOGIT estimates the same logit model as the -logit- command, but with an estimator that gives lower mean square error in the presence of rare events data for coefficients.' The program implements the procedures proposed by King and Zeng (1999a; 1999b).

more people there are in a household, the higher the need for communication and the more devices are needed if the different members want to be able to connect to the Internet at the same time or want to have more independence in their communication. On the other hand, it may be linked to the fact that the cost per person of having a PC and fixed Internet connection is lower in a larger household. Also, if the household is larger, it is more probable that at least one of its members needs to have a PC (e.g. to work or study). Thus, the larger the household is, the lower the probability of having only mobile devices.

Conclusions

The spread of mobile devices increased very quickly in the last couple of years and we can expect that this trend will continue. Therefore, researchers and online panels users have started to pay interest both to the new opportunities and to the new challenges that mobile devices could offer them. Previous research has started to study the spread of the phenomenon by mainly focusing on web coverage, on the mobile penetration in a general population or on the analysis of mobile web usage. The growing interest generated by mobile access and usage of the web is confirmed by some experiments that were implemented about how to adapt questionnaires to these new devices, mainly smartphones and tablets. However, some of the preliminary results are based on only small samples of panelists. Moreover, some countries were not considered in previous research, even if the results can also strongly vary depending on the territorial context. Besides, these phenomena are developing and spreading so quickly that the results from two or three years ago may be already out of date. On the other hand, there is a real demand for more information about these topics from web panels, which have to face the current lack of knowledge and do not know exactly what the best strategies are for the future. That is why, in this chapter, we tried to provide some new evidence about the potential for the use of mobile web in surveys for online commercial panels like Netquest, taking into account different countries not studied in-depth before: Spain, Portugal and some Latin American countries.

Firstly, we have investigated the proportions of panelists who own different devices across different periods and we have seen that, even if the results differ across countries, overall, a very large proportion of panelists own mobile devices, in particular smartphones. This proportion increased quickly in less than one and a half year, whereas the proportion of desktop PC owners tended to decrease. Besides, there is also a non-negligible proportion of panelists who have access regularly to the devices, even though they do not own them. Therefore, a really large proportion of the panelists can be considered as potential mobile web respondents. However, our results also show that a majority of panelists own not only one but a combination of several kinds of devices, PC and mobile. Thus, they really can choose through which device to answer surveys. This means that the preferences for answering surveys using different devices need to be studied to get a more precise idea of the need for mobile surveys. Our results only show that there is a large potential. This potential is also linked to the characteristics of the panelists who own different devices. Comparing different groups of panelists based on their access to mobile devices, we found significant differences in terms of the main background variables (age and education) between respondents who own only a PC versus the others. We also found significant differences between the respondents who own only mobile devices versus the others in terms of education and, in some countries, household size. This all suggests that, even though mobile web respondents may still represent a relatively small group, it is crucial for the representativeness of a survey to include and involve them. Besides, the evolution over time suggests that this group will keep growing very quickly.

Further interesting questions are: how is it possible to implement the adaptation of a survey to a mobile mode in a cost-effective way? And how is it possible to reach this objective while allowing, at the same time, the comparison of results obtained across different devices? Even if the interest for these themes exists already, and even if many studies have been carried on, these are still quite recent and unexplored topics of research, and much more needs to be done about them. Moreover, technology is evolving so quickly that research results also have to be updated more and more frequently to obtain and maintain an up-to-date view of the reality. Therefore, we need longer time series to track the different phenomena in the future. Furthermore, some of the data we used in this work were not specifically planned to be used for that type of analysis when they were collected. This means that we had to adapt the analyses to the information that was available. Nevertheless, in the future, data could be collected in a more systematic way, and data collection could be planned in advance, such that more precise and/or more complete information becomes available. Previous results, including ours, are also focused on a limited number of countries. Research should be extended to more and more contexts, since we have noticed that the situation clearly varies across countries.

Appendix

		Q1-13	Q2-13	Q3-13	Q4-13	Q1-14
Argentina	PC,T	3,513	1,985	328	8,277	3,830
	S	417	1,472	13,220	11,245	2,663
Brazil	PC,T	4,994	8,117	4,149	12,253	15,962
	S	63	75	30,265	1,833	1,930
Chile	PC,T	1,567	1,811	765	7,641	1,578
	S	13	263	2,737	2,903	263

(Continued)

Colombia	PC,T	2,797	3,080	799	7,862	2,935
	S	238	461	5,848	2,804	773
Spain	PC,T	NA	34,493	4,323	63	5,866
	S	783	2,654	218	248	3,817
Mexico	PC,T	16,937	7,133	4,015	1,439	5,463
	S	674	666	7,117	4,535	605
Portugal	PC,T	919	4,596	1,512	266	187
	S	827	136	1,394	3,658	1,281

Appendix 1: Access to mobile devices: number of observations in each country (by quarter-year); Note: PC = desktop + laptop; T = tablet; S = smartphone.

Acknowledgements

The authors would like to acknowledge the contribution of the European Network WebDataNet (COST Action IS1004, http://webdatanet.cbs.dk/). We are also very grateful to Netquest for providing us with the necessary data and to the University of Bergamo (this research has been partially supported by the 60% University funds).

References

Cisco VNI Mobile. (2014). *Cisco Visual Networking Index: Global Mobile Data Traffic Forecast Update, 2013–2018.* Retrieved October 2014 from http://www.cisco.com/c/en/us/solutions/collateral/service-provider/visual-networking-index-vni/white_paper_c11-520862.html

de Bruijne, M., & Wijnant, A. (2013). Comparing survey results obtained via mobile devices and computers: An experiment with a mobile web survey on a heterogeneous group of mobile devices versus a computer assisted web survey. *Social Science Computer Review, 31,* 483–505.DOI: http://dx.doi.org/10.1177/0894439313483976

Eurobarometer. (2012). *E-Communication Household Survey - Special Eurobarometer 381 report.* Retrieved October 2014 from http://ec.europa.eu/public_opinion/archives/ebs/ebs_381_en.pdf

Fuchs, M., & Busse, B. (2009). The coverage bias of mobile web surveys across European countries. *International Journal of Internet Science, 4,* 21–33.

Internet World Stats. (2014). Retrieved July and September 2014 from http://www.internetworldstats.com

King, G., & Zeng, L. (1999a). *Logistic Regression in Rare Events Data.* Department of Government, Harvard University. Retrieved from http://GKing.Harvard.Edu

King, G., & Zeng, L. (1999b). *Estimating Absolute, Relative, and Attributable Risks in Case-Control Studies.* Department of Government, Harvard University. Retrieved from http://GKing.Harvard.Edu

KPCB. (2014). *Internet Trends 2014 – Code Conference.* Retrieved October 2014 from http://www.slideshare.net/kleinerperkins/internet-trends-2014-05-28-14-pdf

Nielsen Mobile. (2008). *Critical mass: The worldwide state of the mobile Web.* Nielsen Company.

Okazaki, S. (2007). Assessing mobile-based online surveys: Methodological considerations and pilot study in an advertising context. *International Journal of Market Research, 49,* 651–675.

Smart Insights. (2014). *21 Internet trends from the annual KPCB trends report.* Retrieved October 2014 from http://www.smartinsights.com/digital-marketing-strategy/internet-trends-2014-mary-meeker/

StatCounter Global Stats. (2013). *Mobile vs. desktop.* Retrieved July 2014 from http://gs.statcounter.com/#mobile_vs_desktop-ww-monthly-201201-201309

StatCounter Global Stats. (2014). Retrieved October 2014 from http://gs.statcounter.com/

Statista. (2014). *Global fixed broadband and mobile internet penetration 2008–2017.* Retrieved October 2014 from http://www.statista.com/statistics/280430/worldwide-fixed-broadband-and-mobile-internet-penetration/

Statistics Netherlands. (2012). *Mobile internet use continues to grow.* [Press release], PB12-060, 23 October 2012. Retrieved June 2, 2013, from http://www.cbs.nl/en-GB/menu/themas/vrije-tijd-cultuur/publicaties/artikelen/archief/2012/2012-060-pb.htm

Tomz, M., King, G., & Zeng, L. (1999). RELOGIT: Rare Events Logistic Regression, Version 1.1. Cambridge, MA: Harvard University, October 1. Retrieved from http://gking.harvard.edu/

CHAPTER 9

Willingness of Online Access Panel Members to Participate in Smartphone Application-Based Research

Robert Pinter

Corvinus University of Budapest, Hungary; eNET Internet Research and
Consulting Ltd., Hungary, robert.pinter@enet.hu

Abstract

There are limited academic activities on the methodological aspects of smartphone research applications. This book chapter focuses on this niche area of
research. VeVa (Véleményem Van) is an online / mobile hybrid research panel
which has been running since 2013 in Hungary. VeVa is already suitable for
online research, and its smartphone research application will be available for
panel members from 2015. Download of the application will be part of the
recruitment process as well. The VeVa panel aims to convince both recent and
future panel members to download and use its research application. An online
survey was carried out in October 2014 in the VeVa panel to investigate who is
willing to download the research application and why. A survey was conducted
to evaluate nonresponse bias with an analysis of those panel members who
are not willing to download the application. In this book chapter we analyze
the motivations related to application download, comparing app accepters, app
rejecters and uncertain respondents. This is followed by a detailed analysis of
the three groups to detect differences in their characteristics. We have identified 19 significant variables and found smartphone application usage patterns
as the most important explanation. There are only slight differences between
the groups in regard to socio-demographic variables and to social and other
further analyzed factors.

How to cite this book chapter:
Pinter, R. 2015. Willingness of Online Access Panel Members to Participate in
   Smartphone Application-Based Research. In: Toninelli, D, Pinter, R & de
   Pedraza, P (eds.) *Mobile Research Methods: Opportunities and Challenges of Mobile
   Research Methodologies*, Pp. 141–156. London: Ubiquity Press. DOI: http://dx.doi.
   org/10.5334/bar.i. License: CC-BY 4.0.

Keywords

online research, mobile research, smartphone research, research applications, socio-demographic differences, survey methodology, nonresponse bias

Introduction: exploring smartphone research as a methodological topic

Due to the more frequent use of mobile phones in conducting surveys, new methodological questions have appeared in the world of research. Studies of the last few years have focused on questions such as the role of mobile phones in sampling (Andrews, Russell Bennett & Drennan 2011; Terhanian & Bremer 2012), the impact of smart technology on research (Mace 2012), mixed-mode and multiple devices (Callegaro 2013), mobile web surveys (de Bruijne & Wijnant 2013; Mavletova 2013; Mavletova & Couper 2013) and the effect of the use of mobile devices in a web panel (de Bruijne & Wijnant 2014).

These research papers primarily engaged with the use of mobile phones in web surveys or other more traditional research methods. But mobile phones can be used to participate in research not only by voice or via browsers, but using dedicated smartphone applications for research purposes (and that even offline). There are many smartphone research applications in commercial market research. However, not so many research projects done with applications have compared them with online surveys (CAWI[32]) or other current quantitative methods (CAPI,[33] CATI[34] or PAPI[35]). This is still true even though mobile research (MAWI[36] or MAPI[37]) can be held as the fifth biggest research method besides the former mentioned ones (Snaith 2009). Both in MAWI and in MAPI mobile devices are mainly used in traditional ways and not with smartphone applications (of course there are a few exceptions, for example smartphone applications for data gathering with interviewers, e.g. droid Survey Offline Forms on Android or iSurvey Offline Surveys & Data Collection Forms on iOS).

Use of smartphone research applications is not so common in the academic sphere, despite the fact that these kinds of applications have been available for more than five years (for a first typology of 54 different research applications

---

[32] CAWI – Computer-Assisted Web Interviewing
[33] CAPI – Computer-Assisted Personal Interviewing
[34] CATI – Computer-Assisted Telephone Interviewing
[35] PAPI – Paper-and-Pencil Interviewing
[36] MAWI – Mobile-Assisted Web Interviewing, where a mobile is substituted for the computer.
[37] MAPI – Mobile-Assisted Personal Interviewing, where a mobile is substituted for the computer.

on iPhone and iPad see Michelson 2010[38]). This is probably the main reason why research methodologists have not yet explored smartphone applications as an important topic of investigation on research and other methodological activities. While using mobile applications for data collection researchers should answer the following questions: 1) what are the characteristics of respondents with smartphones compared to those who do not have this device, 2) who is willing to download a research application among them and who is not willing, and finally 3) who participates in research (completes the tasks and questionnaires)?

This paper deals with these questions and applies the example of VeVa (Véleményem Van), a Hungarian online research panel, and its new research application which will be introduced in 2015. Based on Michelson (2010)'s classification, the VeVa smartphone research app is mainly for surveys. However, it can be applied for diary, ethnographic and location based research as well. The targets are consumers (members of the VeVa panel), the access is closed (available only for members: a user needs a username and password to login) and the app can be downloaded for free.

VeVa is an online / mobile hybrid research system in Hungary that has been running since 2013. Its explicit goal is to allow members to participate in traditional online surveys as well as in research through a smartphone application. Online research projects have been carried out since early 2014. The system will be ready for smartphone application research in 2015, with the involvement of panel members as respondents. Wide-scale internal testing of research applications has been running since 2014 with the help of panel members. The panel already had 15,000 members at the beginning of 2015, before the introduction of the research application. The long-range goal of VeVa is to collect 50,000 members, but only after the research application becomes available in app stores[39] and the download of the application becomes integrated into the recruitment process. In order to make the integration as smooth as possible preparative research was carried out in October 2014 among VeVa panel members. This study investigated the attitude of smartphone owners, in terms of their willingness to download the application. It also examined how the application will be used in various research types in the future (e.g. surveys, diaries, ethnographic studies, location based research projects and short mobile surveys).

This research on attitudes had several objectives. First, it seeks to understand the characteristics of those panel members who would download the research application and to identify their interests in certain research types. Second, it seeks to see if there is any difference between those panel members who would

---

[38] Michelson (2010)'s research app categories were the following: survey, qualitative, mystery shopping, panel and other research apps, helpful non-research apps.
[39] The VeVa smartphone research application will be first published on Android, then on iOS, and finally as a Windows Phone app.

download the research application and those who would not. Third, it aims to find out what is the reason behind the 'rejection' attitude and what arguments can be provided to convince those who are not willing to download the app. Fourth, it seeks to find out what the recommendation of this research could be with regard to the integration of the research application into the VeVa panel recruitment process, as well as the expected use of the research application. In this chapter I shortly present the results of this research and try to answer the above questions.

Background and hypotheses: an exploratory research

The research was designed primarily for exploratory purposes. We wanted to examine what variables have correlations with willingness to download the research applications. Three groups of these variables were identified: socio-demographic variables, smartphone and application using habits, and other background variables. The first two are obvious choices, but we had to define the third groups.

Biler, Šenk and Winklerová (2013) found that the non-technical parameters of religion, use of shopping or of travel discount cards, and charity had a significant impact on participation in a study with GPS devices in the Czech Republic. We therefore included background variables in our questionnaire based on our hypotheses that willingness to download the research app may increase with the possession of loyalty cards and with frequency of legal gambling activities by respondents. We also assumed that research app downloading preferences may have a connection with free-time activities, with religion and with political orientation.

One of the explicit goals of this research was to understand the concerns of smartphone owners regarding the download of the research application. We investigated what would be the relevant answer to these concerns to be capable to adjust the recruitment process later based on this feedback.

Data collection

The online survey research was carried out in October 2014 among VeVa panel members on their attitudes toward downloading a smartphone research application.[40] The sample size was relatively big (N = 2028) compared to the total size of the panel (~15,000). This survey has taken into account the usual response rate in VeVa online surveys (~30%), and the actual response rate was 26%. The bigger-than-usual sample size was intentional because we planned to

---

[40] I would like to thank for their work my colleagues at eNET, namely Tünde Hujber, Balázs Molnár and Géza Schneider, who have collaborated in this research project and helped to prepare the questionnaire, carry out the research and analyze the results.

form different groups with the respondents to address further questions during the survey study. We used a quota method for sampling from the panel (gender, age and region quotas) in order to make our findings follow the structure of the Hungarian adult (older than 18-years-old) population.

The questionnaire contained eight sections altogether, which were the following in the order of sections (see **Figure 1**):

1. '**Section S**' was submitted to everyone and contained only one question to screen out those who do not have *Smartphones* and who therefore cannot download the research application even if they would like to (these participants skipped most of the sections and completed only the final 'Section B').
2. '**Section SO**' was submitted only to *Smartphone Owners* and contained 14 questions. Part of the questions sought out basic data about smartphone devices, e.g. for how long the respondents had had smartphones, the types of operation systems and brands of their smartphones, and the respondents' application downloading habits in general. The other part of the questions focused on participating habits in online research with mobile devices.
3. '**Section D**' contained only one screening question about whether the respondent would *Download* the dedicated research application of the VeVa online panel in the future.
4. '**Section P**' was submitted only to those smartphone owners who responded *Positively* and reported they were willing to download the application (this group was referred to later as 'app accepters'). This section had seven questions: how often and for how long they would participate in smartphone research; what would motivate them to download the research application; what was their preferred types of incentives; and what was their possible future participation in short surveys, location based research, diary, ethnographic studies, passive measurement[41] and research triggered by a smartphone sensor.
5. '**Section U-N**' was submitted only to those smartphone owners who were *Uncertain* or *Negative* about whether they would download the research application of VeVa. It contained only two questions. In the first one we showed eight different statements (possible concerns or barriers) about the research application, and respondents were asked to rate them on a scale of 1 to 4. Then we showed our concrete replies to those concerns/statements which had been rated as 3 or 4 by the respondent earlier. After this we asked in the second question whether they had changed their minds and would download the research application of the VeVa panel.

---

[41] We have asked this question despite the fact that the VeVa application is not capable of doing passive measurement (i.e. of investigating background phone activities with the consent of participants).

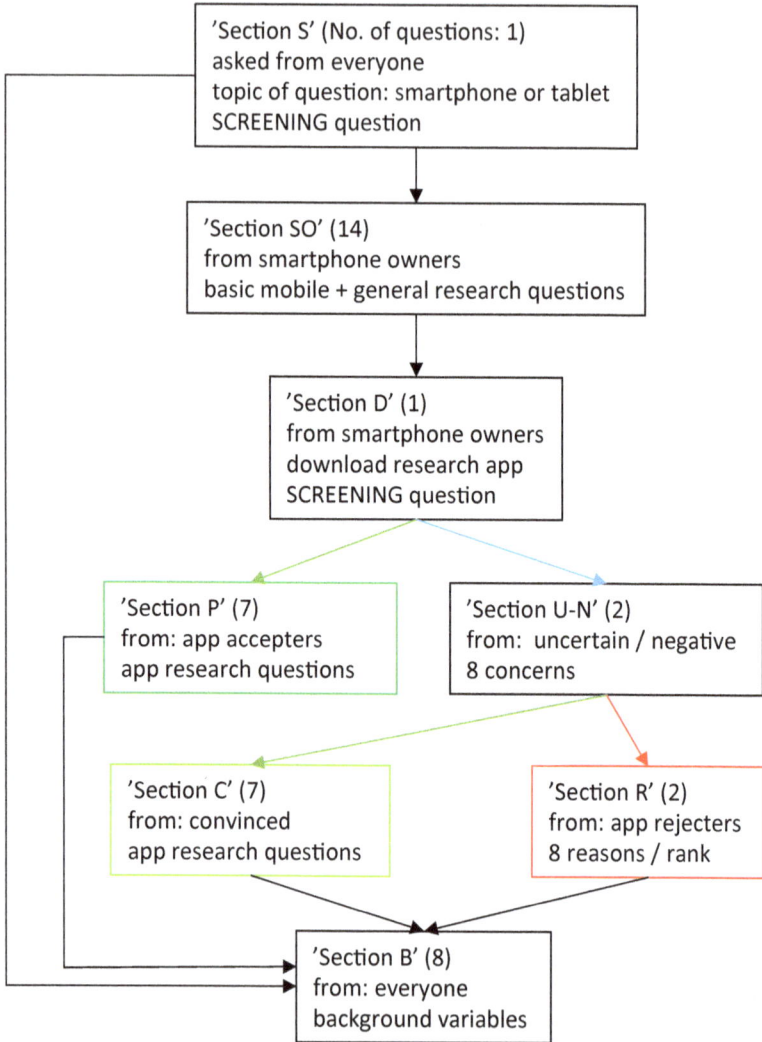

Figure 1: Structure of survey questionnaire on willingness to download the smartphone research application of the VeVa online panel (name of section, number of questions in brackets, respondent group to whom it was submitted, topics of questions).

6. **'Section C'** was submitted to those smartphone owners who were previously uncertain or negative, but whom our arguments *Convinced* and who had changed their minds and now replied that they would download the research application. 'Section C' also contained seven questions, but

it was a shorter version of 'Section P' (the reason for the shortening was to decrease the possible attrition rate because of grid questions and the longer path of this group in the questionnaire).

7. **'Section R'** was submitted to those smartphone owners who were previously uncertain or negative and whom our arguments could not convince. They finally *Rejected* the download of the application (this group is referred to later as 'app rejecters' and 'uncertain'). This section contained two questions. In the first one we showed eight possible reasons for rejecting the research application, and respondents could choose a maximum of three and rank them. The second question was an open question for those who had chosen other, non-listed reasons for rejection in the first question, so that they could specify their reasons with their own words.

8. **'Section B'** was submitted again to everyone (including those who were screened out in the initial 'Section S'). It contained eight *Background* variables used for later analyses: how often and for what reason did respondents replace mobile phones; possession of loyalty cards; regularity of legal gambling; regularity of going out; preference for passive or active free-time activities; religion (religious or non-religious); and political orientation (left or right).

Socio-demographic variables (such as age, gender, region, settlement type, education, income etc.) were imported from panel variables based on replies given by respondents in a former recruitment process, hence we did not need to ask them again and the questionnaire could be shorter.

Research results

Accepters, rejecters and uncertain respondents: motivations for participation and reasons of rejection

61% of respondents (N = 1227) had smartphones within our sample. 21% of smartphone owners (N = 257) had already used their mobile devices to fill in 'traditional' online questionnaires earlier, but not a smartphone research app. Altogether, 10% of panel members 'filled in questionnaires of market research companies' by mobile, which is a relatively high percentage; however, it is in line with the international literature (Bosnjak et al. 2012; Jue 2015).[42]

About 42% of smartphone owners reported they were willing to download the research application (accepters), 35% rejected it and 23% were uncertain (N = 1227).

---

[42] It means that those members of VeVa who regularly fill in online market research questionnaires by smartphone represent 10% of the full panel (61% of panel members have a smartphone, 21% of them have filled in online questionnaires by mobile, and 78% of these 21% of smartphone using respondents replied in market research projects).

Motivation of accepters

What would motivate the first accepters (N = 510) to download the application? Motivations would be the following ones for them – with multiple responses option: 80% chose incentives (prizes); 47% were interested in innovations (we may say that it is the impact of novelty[43]); 43% would like to have impact on products and services by expressing opinions in smartphone research projects; 37% like to fill in questionnaires; and 36% would like to tell their opinion.

It means that two of the top three motivations mentioned are classical ones of the type which also motivated our panel members to join the panel itself earlier, and only the second argument (interested in innovations) is something which has a strong connection with the nature of the smartphone research application.

Reasons for rejection

The reasons for uncertainty or rejection in the first round given in 'Section U-N' (N = 717) were – as proportions of those who rated the given reason with 3 or 4 on a 1–4 scale:

- there is not enough **free time** to participate in mobile research: 61%
- there is not enough **information** to decide about the use of the research application: 53%
- an expectation that use of the research application can cause **extra costs** (most probably because of limited mobile broadband plan of respondents): 45%
- would **participate** only in some research projects but less likely in others: 44%
- afraid that use of the research application would heavily drain **battery** of smartphone: 43%

After asking about the reasons for rejection we gave respondents specific information regarding their previously chosen concerns. Therefore, in 'Section U-N' 27% of rejecters and uncertain respondents could be convinced to download the application, but 28% of them remained uncertain and 45% again rejected the download of the research app.

The main reasons for rejection in the second round (N = 502) were – as cumulated percentage of mentions as first, second and third reasons:

- there is not enough **free time** to participate in mobile research: 63%
- there is not enough **information** to decide about the use of the research application: 38%

---

[43] The VeVa smartphone research application is the first of its kind available to Hungarian respondents, hence it may have some novelty to panel members.

- other: 37% (N = 134). Small screen size (N = 36), prefers computer to fill in questionnaires (N = 21), smartphone is used mainly for voice calls (N = 13).
- afraid that use of research application would heavily drain **battery** of smartphone: 32%
- would **participate** only in some research projects but less likely in others: 30%

Significant correlation between downloading research application and other variables

Altogether, 57% of smartphone owners were convinced in the first and second rounds to download the smartphone research application of VeVa, 27% rejected the app permanently and 16% remained uncertain at the end. So the majority of the sample was open to the research app. Every sixth respondent could be convinced with more information and more relevant arguments. And only approximately one quarter was reluctant to participate in smartphone application based research.

We have compared these three groups – accepters, rejecters, uncertain – in order to see which variables show significant correlation with willingness to download the research application. We wanted to identify significant differences between these three groups and find explanations of why respondents accepted or rejected the application or remained uncertain.

Table 1 summarizes the results of significant correlations between variables and willingness to download the research application. We did not find any variable with a strong correlation, and we found only four variables with medium levels of correlation. Every other variable had a weak or very weak correlation.

Smartphone using habits

The following variables have a significant correlation with the three groups and the willingness to download the application:[44]

- medium correlation:
  - how often respondent downloads applications (more regular app downloaders are open to research app, majority of non-downloaders reject it)
  - total number of applications on smartphone (non-linear connection)
  - number of applications regularly used (the more apps used, the more willingness to download the research app)
  - how often respondent used GPS on smartphone (more openness to research app if GPS is more often used)

---

[44] The majority of our variables have no connection with the willingness to download the research application, and we do not list them here. However, it is important to mention that ownership of loyalty cards is among them from the previously highlighted background variables.

Variable	Type	Chi² (significant values)	Cramer's V	Level of connection correlation
How often download applications to their smartphone	application	0.000	0.263	medium
Number of applications regularly used	application	0.000	0.221	medium
Used to fill in questionnaires on smartphone	survey habits	0.000	0.209	medium
Total number of applications on smartphone	application	0.001	0.200	medium
How often have used GPS on smartphone	smartphone	0.000	0.189	weak
Labor market status	economic	0.000	0.164	weak
Type of smartphone operation system	smartphone	0.000	0.163	weak
Age	socio-demo	0.000	0.159	weak
Brand of smartphone	smartphone	0.000	0.150	weak
Monthly personal income	economic	0.017	0.144	weak
Replacement frequency of smartphone	smartphone	0.000	0.136	weak
Political orientation	social	0.001	0.136	weak
How often socialize, meeting with friends, relatives or colleagues	social	0.000	0.131	weak
Active or passive free time activities preferred	social	0.000	0.129	weak
For how long have had smartphone	smartphone	0.003	0.109	weak
Have a tablet	technical	0.000	0.106	weak
Frequency of gambling	social / econ.	0.030	0.090	very weak
Main earner	socio-demo	0.048	0.090	very weak
Religion	social	0.035	0.089	very weak

Table 1: Variables with significant correlation to download of the research application.

If Cramer's V = 0.2 to 0.5, medium correlation; 0.1 to 0.2, weak correlation; below 0.1, very weak correlation.

- used to fill in questionnaires on smartphone (more open to app if already filled in questionnaires by mobile)
- weak correlation:
  - respondent has a tablet
  - for how long respondent has had a smartphone (the longer has had smartphone, the more open to the research app)
  - type of smartphone operation system (smartphone owners with iOS are more open to the app)
  - brand of smartphone (iPhone and HTC owners are more open to the app than the others)
  - replacement frequency of smartphone (non-linear connection)
  - how often does respondent socialize, meeting with friends, relatives or colleagues (the more often they socialize, the more open they are to the app)
  - active or passive free-time activities preferred (non-linear connection)
  - political orientation (non-linear connection)
- very weak connection:
  - frequency of gambling (non-linear connection)
  - religion (non-religious smartphone owners are a bit less open to research app)

Summarizing the findings we found that general application using habits are the utmost determining factors for the research app downloading preferences: if someone often downloads applications, uses them regularly and already has plenty of apps on their smartphone, they will more likely download the research app and give it a chance. However, these connections are still medium strong only. Former survey filling experiences also help to convince respondents that it is worthwhile to download the application.

Socio-demographic profile

Beside the variables analyzed above certain socio-demographic variables also have a correlation with the willingness to download the research application. It is important to see what kind of socio-demographic differences we have between the three groups:

- weak connection: age (with increasing age the willingness to download the app decreases); monthly personal income (respondents with no personal income are more open[45]); labor market status (students are more open to the research app, while pensioners are less open)

---

[45] Most probably respondents with no personal income are students who are usually experienced with smartphones (N.B. the sample contained only adults, older than 18). This is reinforced by the significant connection in labor market status.

- very weak connection: main earner (more willingness to download the app if respondent is not the main earner in the household)
- no connection: gender; region; settlement type (i.e. capital city, county seat, city, village or other); education; marital status; main shopper of the household; number of children younger than 18 in the household; monthly household income; size of household; and subjective income status.

Discussion and conclusion

There are not enough experiments yet in the academic sphere on the methodological problems of running projects with smartphone research applications. That is why this research and these results could be interesting and useful for a wider audience. The main results of the research carried out with VeVa panel members on their willingness to download the research application of the panel are described below.

Reasons for rejection: 'more information is needed'

The reasons for rejection show that the panel members do not have enough information about the nature and functionality of the VeVa smartphone research application. We need to provide more information before asking to download the real app. Participation in mobile research is usually less time consuming than filling in a traditional online questionnaire (a mobile questionnaire is rarely longer than 8–10 minutes, while a traditional online questionnaire is rarely shorter than 8–10 minutes). From this perspective 'there is not enough free time' is a fear rather than a real barrier, especially if we keep in mind that these respondents are already members of an online research panel and actively participate in online research, so that they surely have free time to spend on research questions.

'There isn't enough information' as the second argument also convinced us that more information is necessary, and some respondents feel the same. Misbelief concerning extra costs was also derived from lack of information: the application is built in a way that means it works offline as well and uses only WiFi Internet connection by default. Of course respondents can change the settings and use 3G or 4G (mobile broadband) if they wish. Occasional participation in research as justification to reject the app download seemed to be strange. Participation in VeVa research projects has always been voluntary, and this is highlighted in every research invitation e-mail. This would not be different in projects run by smartphone research application. However, respondents need to be reassured that the rule of volunteering will not be changed with introduction of the app. The last reason of fast battery drain is also based on lack of information – however, one needs to try the application before this concern can really be disproved.

In the first round 42% of respondents were willing to download the VeVa smartphone research application, but after giving relevant information to the other participants, a further 15% were convinced. Meanwhile, the ratio of app rejecters decreased from 35% to 27%, and in the case of uncertain members it decreased from 23% to 16%, so it was possible to win supporters for the application from both groups.

In the main reasons for rejection in the second round, 'not enough free time' remained almost the same as in the first round (63% compared to 61% in the first round). This is possibly a good choice for some respondents to reject the application in a polite way, but this result also shows that our argument about volunteer participation was not convincing.

'Not enough information' decreased from 53% to 38%, which is understandable: those respondents who felt the received extra information was enough most probably were convinced and did not need to reply to the questions in this section. However, the fact that information scarcity is still the second barrier in the second round warns us that certain groups need more information about the application in advance. It is worthwhile to investigate this topic further, possibly with qualitative research methods.

'Other' as third reason in the second round also highlighted an important message: we did not think about every concern when we designed the questionnaire, so this result was very important. It would be a good idea to add the three new insights (small screen size, prefers computer to fill in questionnaires, smartphone is used mainly for voice calls) to the original list of eight arguments when we integrate the download of the application into our recruitment process.

The fact that a few arguments were not among the top five shows that these factors are less important for the majority of rejecters, and more important for researchers and VeVa system designers. However, it does not mean that these concerns can be neglected. A smartphone research application can be used for observation only with the consent of users. Personal data and responses must be used with care and under clear rules in a research environment. Finally, the application needs to be user friendly and simple to use. We would suggest that these factors represent a certain kind of minimum expectations (of respondents) that research apps must fulfill per se.

Considering the reasons for rejection provided, it is clear that prior to download more information is needed about the research application for the panel members. But most probably it is also true that it is worthwhile to choose carefully whom to inform, when and with what kind of information about the application and its expected use. Doing it the right way can improve the conversion rate and mitigate the fear arising from the uncertainty of the possible downloaders.

Slight differences only in socio-demographic profile; and smartphone using habits as decisive

It is an important lesson from the research that there is little difference between app accepters, app rejecters and uncertain respondent from a socio-demographic point of view. This is good news for the broad applicability of research application in the future.

Nineteen variables have been identified during the research as significant ones, and they have medium, weak or very weak connection to the willingness groups. Nearly half of these variables are related to smartphones and their use. Smartphone application related habits (e.g. how often someone downloads applications, number of regularly used apps, total number of apps on smartphone) have the biggest impact on the willingness to download the research app. Social factors such as religious or political orientation, leisure time preferences or gambling habits have only weak connections to the three groups, so these factors most probably will not distort the sampling process and the results of future smartphone application based studies.

The results regarding the socio-demographic profiles mean at least two things: first, we need to find other variables if we want to explain why certain panel members are open to our smartphone research app and others are uncertain or reject it. Second, this result is a very good news from a smartphone research perspective: smartphone application based research can be carried out without the fear that participants are completely different in socio-demographic categories from those smartphone owners who do not want to participate in this kind of research. Socio-demographic characteristics of app accepters are somewhat, but not very, different from those of rejecters or uncertain respondents: they are a bit younger and more likely to be students with no personal income.

From the other 15 variables (with weak and very weak correlations), 5 are related to smartphones and 1 is technical. Altogether, nearly half (9 out of 19) identified variables are smartphone centered. Four variables are socio-demographic (two of them are economic) and five are social. From the previously incorporated social background variables, five proved to be a good decision and have correlation to the willingness of application download. However, these relationships are weak or very weak. Social factors are far less decisive than the already mentioned smartphone ones, or even than the socio-demographic ones. This can be considered again as good news. Research application accepters are only slightly different from app rejecters and uncertain respondents in their political views, religious attitudes, leisure time preferences or gambling activities.

Finally, it is quite sure that there are countless topics for smartphone application related research in the future. In the short term a possible topic can be, for example, the impact of different incentives on the willingness to download the application. The impact of other advantages when downloading the application (and the measure of the difference between the conditions) can also be an important variable. Finally we may focus on the investigation of privacy concerns and other factors with different wording at application download and with a measure of the impact of such different wording on the conversion rate.

Acknowledgements

I would like to thank Aigul Mavletova and Emese Burjan for the comments they made to a former version of this book chapter.

References

Andrews, L., Russell Bennett, R., & Drennan, J. (2011). Capturing affective experiences using the SMS Experience Sampling (SMS-ES) method. *International Journal of Market Research*, *53*(4), 479–506. DOI: http://dx.doi.org/10.2501/IJMR-53-4-479-506

Biler, S., Šenk, P., & Winklerová, L. (2013). *Willingness of Individuals to Participate in a Travel Behavior Survey Using GPS Devices*. Paper presented at the NTTS 2013 – New Techniques and Technologies for Statistics Conference. Retrieved April 5, 2015, from http://www.cros-portal.eu/sites/default/files/NTTS2013fullPaper_234.pdf

Bosnjak, M., Becker, K. R., Poggio, T., Funke, F., Wachenfeld, A., & Fischer, B. (2012, November). *Mobile survey participation rates in commercial market research: A meta-analysis*. Paper presented at the 6th Internet Survey Methods Workshop, Ljubljana, Slovenia.

Callegaro, M. (2013). From mixed-mode to multiple devices. *International Journal of Market Research*, *55*(2), 317–320. DOI: http://dx.doi.org/10.2501/IJMR-2013-026

de Bruijne, M., & Wijnant, A. (2013). Comparing Survey Results Obtained via Mobile Devices and Computers: An Experiment With a Mobile Web Survey on a Heterogeneous Group of Mobile Devices Versus a Computer-Assisted Web Survey. *Social Science Computer Review*, *31*(4), 482–504. DOI: http://dx.doi.org/10.1177/0894439313483976

de Bruijne, M., & Wijnant, A. (2014). Mobile Response in Web Panels. *Social Science Computer Review*, *32*(6), 728–742. DOI: http://dx.doi.org/10.1177/0894439314525918

Jue, A. (2015). *Mobile Participation in Online Surveys*. Decipher WHITE PAPER - Trends Report. Retrieved April 5, 2015, from http://ww2.focusvision.com/wp-content/uploads/2015/03/FV_Dec_MobileUpdateWhite-Paper.pdf

Mace, T. (2012). Developments and the impact of smart technology. *International Journal of Market Research*, *54*(4), 567–570. DOI: http://dx.doi.org/10.2501/IJMR-54-4-567-570

Mavletova, A. M. (2013). Data Quality in PC and Mobile Web Surveys. *Social Science Computer Review*, *31*(6), 725–743. DOI: http://dx.doi.org/10.1177/0894439313485201

Mavletova, A., & Couper, M. P. (2013). Sensitive topics in PC Web and mobile web surveys: Is there a difference? *Survey Research Methods*, *7*(3), 191–205.

Michelson, M. (2010, December). *There is an app for that! A review of smartphone apps for marketing research.* Paper presented at the International conference on Market Research in the Mobile World, Berlin, Germany. Retrieved April 04, 2015, from https://app.box.com/s/27ca01dbe9a2f1ab9081/1/295759904/2342922278/1

Snaith, T. (2009, August). Mobile research – the fifth methodology? *Quirk's Marketing Research Review*, p. 26. Retrieved April 04, 2015, from http://www.quirks.com/articles/2009/20090803.aspx?searchID=112361877&sort=5&pg=5

Terhanian, G., & Bremer, J. (2012). A smarter way to select respondents for surveys? *International Journal of Market Research*, *54*(6), 751–780. DOI: http://dx.doi.org/10.2501/IJMR-54-6-751-780